CITYSPOTS
SINGA

WHAT'S IN YOUR GUIDEBOOK?

Independent authors Impartial up-to-date information from our travel experts who meticulously source local knowledge.

Experience Thomas Cook's 165 years in the travel industry and guidebook publishing enriches every word with expertise you can trust.

Travel know-how Contributions by thousands of staff around the globe, each one living and breathing travel.

Editors Travel-publishing professionals, pulling everything together to craft a perfect blend of words, pictures, maps and design.

You, the traveller We deliver a practical, no-nonsense approach to information, geared to how you really use it.

CITYSPOTS
SINGAPORE

Pat Levy

Thomas
Cook

Written by Pat Levy
Original photography by Pat Levy
Front cover photography ©Jon Hicks/Corbis
Series design based on an original concept by Studio 183 Limited

Produced by Cambridge Publishing Management Limited
Project Editor: Catherine Burch
Layout: Donna Pedley
Maps: PC Graphics
Transport map: © Communicarta Limited

Published by Thomas Cook Publishing
A division of Thomas Cook Tour Operations Limited
Company Registration No. 1450464 England
PO Box 227, Coningsby Road
Peterborough PE3 8SB, United Kingdom
email: books@thomascook.com
www.thomascookpublishing.com
+ 44 (0) 1733 416477
ISBN: 978-1-84157-825-5

First edition © 2007 Thomas Cook Publishing
Text © 2007 Thomas Cook Publishing
Maps © 2007 Thomas Cook Publishing
Project Editor: Kelly Anne Pipes
Production/DTP: Steven Collins

Printed and bound in Spain by GraphyCems

CONTENTS

CITYSPOTS

SYMBOLS KEY

The following symbols are used throughout this book:

ⓐ address ❶ telephone ⓦ website address ⓔ email
🄻 opening times Ⓝ public transport connections ❶ important

The following symbols are used on the maps:

𝑖	information office	O	city
✈	airport	O	large town
✚	hospital	○	small town
🄲	police station	=	motorway
🄱	bus station	—	main road
🄴	railway station		minor road
Ⓜ	MRT	—	railway
✝	cathedral		

❶ numbers denote featured cafés & restaurants

Hotels and restaurants are graded by approximate price
as follows:

£ budget ££ mid-range £££ expensive

▶ Singapore's skyline

INTRODUCING
Singapore

Introduction

There's a kind of unreal quality to your first few minutes in Singapore. You will probably arrive at the end of a long-haul flight feeling a little jaded, and it is blissful to glide calmly through the air-conditioned atmosphere of the arrivals lounge. But beware: its vast size and the bustle of people can have a soporific effect, making you unready for the moment you exit into the real atmosphere of the place and have the sudden feeling of being slapped in the face by a hot wet face flannel.

However, that will be your biggest shock because Singapore works – the cliché is that it works too well – and this helps make it the perfect short-stay destination. On shiny new public transport (don't put your feet up on the seats, eat or drink or, heavens forefend, drop your bubble gum on the floor) or in a swanky limousine you will cruise through the manicured expressways – no one exceeding the speed limit – to the perfect city, a wonderful amalgam of the so new they haven't taken the wrapping off yet and the beautifully preserved and renovated buildings and streets of old.

Everything you ever wanted is here – great hotels, courteous staff, bedazzling food options, shops and exotic markets, nightclubs, history, and a brief ride away raw nature with fabulous animals and plants, tiny unspoiled islands, sandy beaches and an entire island dedicated to fun.

If it's sun you want, there's more than enough and most afternoons a blessed 10-minute shower hits the place to cool it all down. If you don't like the heat, with a bit of planning you need never step outside yet still have fun. If all that sounds a bit Stepford, rest assured that, while you might go crazy if you had to live here for long, a holiday here is just perfect.

⬥ The glitz of Singapore at night

When to go

SEASONS & CLIMATE

Only 136 km (85 miles) north of the equator, Singapore has no seasons; it is hot and humid all year round. Temperatures rarely fall below 21°C (70°F) and peak at around 32°C (90°F) or a little more. Humidity is around 90 per cent. Rain is a regular part of most days, falling in a burst often accompanied by thunderstorms and lasting between 30 minutes and two hours. December and January tend to be a little wetter than other months.

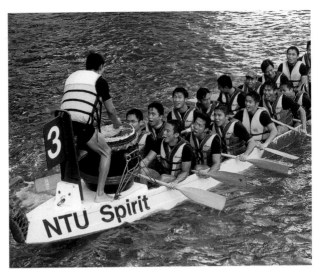

● *Singapore's Dragon Boat Festival is a great spectacle*

ANNUAL EVENTS

January

New Year Suntec City and Sentosa are the places to be, with firework displays, street performers and more.

February

Chinese New Year For several weeks leading up to the event there are decorations and lights around the city. Children are given red envelopes containing money, and families go visiting. On the river there is a celebration of the signs of the Chinese zodiac, featuring whichever animal is in ascendance in that particular year. On New Year's Day the Chingay Parade travels from City Hall to Suntec City and features street performers, acrobats, dragon dance troupes, beauty queens and gymnastic displays from all over the world. On New Year's Day the shops and sights are likely to be closed.

Thaipusam (see pages 14–15).

March–April

Qing Ming Festival Families visit temples to light offerings and bring food to their ancestors. The best place to observe the ceremonies is Kong Meng San Phor Kark See Temple at Sin Ming Road.

May–June

Dragon Boat Festival Rice dumplings are sold all over town and rowers compete in the dragon boat races across Marina Bay.

Vesak Day Celebration of the birth of the Buddha. Temples release caged birds and there are candlelit processions in the evening.

August–September
Festival of the Hungry Ghosts For a month bad spirits are released from hell and walk the earth. To appease them, incense, fake banknotes and paper replicas of consumer goods are burned and offerings of food are made in little makeshift shrines all over the city. There are lots of Chinese street operas throughout the month.
Moon Cake Festival (variable, usually September) Moon cakes are sold all over the city and children carry paper lanterns. Best seen in the Chinese Gardens in Jurong, where enormous lanterns are on display and dragon dances and other performances take place.
National Day Grand multicultural parade followed by speeches and fireworks at the National Stadium.
Womad Four days of concerts and performances in Fort Canning Park.

October–November
Deepavali The Hindu Festival of Lights. Serangoon Road is filled with street markets and bazaars, prayers in the temples, and lots and lots of lights.
Festival of the Nine Emperor Gods Procession in Serangoon Road from the Kiu Ong Yiah Temple. Opera performances and spirit mediums accompany the effigies of the gods.
Navarathiri This month-long Hindu festival sees performances of classical dance and music in Hindu temples all over the city, but especially at the Sri Thandayuthapani Temple on Tank Road. On the final evening a procession led by a silver horse travels around the city.

Ramadan The Muslim month of fasting. In the evenings at sundown when the fast is broken there are stalls around the mosques selling delicacies. Best visited at The Sultan Mosque in Arab Street or in Geylang. The last day of Ramadan, Hari Raya Puasa, is celebrated with new clothes and visits to family.
Thimithi Hindu devotees run barefoot across hot coals at the Sri Mariamman Temple in Chinatown.

December
Christmas Day Tinsel, Chinese Santas, Rudolph, lights and parcels. No change there then.
Hari Raya Haji The celebration of the return of devotees from Mecca.

PUBLIC HOLIDAYS

New Year's Day 1 January
Chinese New Year late January/early February (variable)
Good Friday March/April (variable)
Labour Day 1 May
Vesak Day May (variable)
National Day 9 August

Deepavali October/ November (variable)
Hari Raya Puasa October/ November (variable)
Hari Raya Haji December (variable)
Christmas Day 25 December

13

Thaipusam

Thaipusam takes place in late January/early February in the Hindu month of Thai when the constellation of Pusam is in the ascendant. The festival is practised all over Malaysia but has been banned in India.

● *A devotee at Thaipusam*

The celebration honours the story of Iduban, a devotee of the Lord Murugan who decided to show his love for the god by climbing a mountain carrying offerings of milk and honey. Murugan chose to put obstacles in his path. Despite this, Iduban reached the top and was given a place in heaven at the god's side.

Devotees – often those who wish to ask the god for something (good health, passing an exam, children) – imitate Iduban's journey by walking from the Sri Srinivasa Perumal Temple (see page 81) in Serangoon Road to the Chettiar Temple in Tank Road. The stunning, not to say shocking, manner in which they do this makes this the strangest yet most compelling festival in the city.

Devotees (mostly men) do this ritual at least twice, preparing themselves for weeks in advance with a special diet, abstinence from comforts and special prayers. Entering into a trance-like state, they pierce their mouths with skewers, hang pots of milk and honey by hooks from their flesh and carry huge steel frames called *kavadis* on their shoulders, held in place by more skewers and hooks.

The whole family turns out to help the devotee on their way and shower them with turmeric-coloured water, milk and honey. The long walk in Singapore's oppressive heat lasts for several hours.

❶ Devotees are happy to be photographed (or perhaps they don't notice). Also, you can go into the Sri Srinivasa Perumal Temple to watch the preparations or stand along the route and admire the dedication of the devotees and their families.

History

Singapore's history begins around the 14th century with records of the island, named Temasek, as a small trading post on a swampy, malaria- and tiger-infested island.

Fought over by Javanese and Thai empires, the island languished then until 1819 when the Briton Thomas Stamford Raffles, impressed by the possibilities its deep water bay and wide river mouth offered, decided that this would be a good place for a trading post. Negotiations with the sultan of Melaka were followed by a massive immigration of workers, chiefly from China, for the emerging docks.

By 1824 the island was bought outright and in 1867 it became part of the British Crown Colony called the Straits Settlements. Grand buildings arose, areas of land were earmarked for each of the ethnic communities and by the end of the 19th century Singapore dominated trade in the region.

All was going well until World War II changed things forever. Singapore became a strategic military outpost, holding the line against the encroaching Japanese armies cycling down through the Malay peninsula. The British surrendered the island in 1942. There followed some legendary cruelties on behalf of the occupying forces, murdering as many as 25,000 Chinese men and interning and causing the deaths from disease and malnutrition of hundreds of Allied soldiers and European civilians.

In 1945 the British sheepishly took back what was theirs, but things were never the same. During the 1950s various groups in Malaya began a struggle for independence from Britain, which they achieved in 1957. Singapore was still British but now had an elected legislature and, in 1959, after Lee Kuan Yew's People's Action Party took the majority of seats, it joined the Malay Federation.

By 1965 Singapore was asked to leave by the other states after racial and political tensions led to riots between Chinese and Malays. Singapore suddenly found itself an independent state and despite all the odds – no natural resources, few industries – went from strength to economic strength, developing its port facilities, financial services, IT industry and refineries; building swathes of roads, public housing and hospitals; and creating a compulsory system of social welfare contributions (the Central Provident Fund) for every citizen. It also had massive artistic and political censorship, population control policies that worked too well (threatening the Chinese with becoming fewer in relation to other ethnic groups) and no opposition parties to speak of.

ⓘ Modern Singapore has lightened up a little – although locals laugh ruefully at some of the legislation they live with every day. There are enforced fines for littering, using chewing gum, jaywalking, urinating in lifts and eating on the MRT (Mass Rapid Transit) and there are still large numbers of people executed by the state each year.

Lifestyle

What a strange country Singapore is. From the moment you step out of the airport everything is manicured and well behaved, and everything, it seems at times, has a price. Those Singaporeans who buy into the system laughingly admit to the mantra of the 5Cs: cash, condo, career, car, credit card. A sixth 'C' – children – comes a long way down the line.

The young, upwardly mobile Singaporean is well educated, has a shopping list of requirements and a timetable. Many have little or no time for a social life and, particularly Chinese 20-somethings, attend government sponsored get-togethers where they can meet partners with a similar shopping list to their own. Around 13 per cent of Singaporeans are millionaires and fewer than half of the population were born on the island.

Once in charge of their condo, credit card and car, Singaporeans have time to start enjoying life a little more. Many employ a maid from Indonesia or the Philippines. Eating out is not part of their mantra, it being more like an essential such as breathing or shopping. Most Singaporeans greet their friends with the expression 'Have you eaten?' rather than 'Hello'.

Everyone in Singapore, regardless of income, has strong opinions on places to eat out – where the best hawker centres (see page 28) are, where the best *laksa* can be found, who makes the flakiest *roti*, which pizza place allows you to stack up your salad bowl highest and which all-you-can-eat buffets don't weigh the food you leave on your plate and charge you for it.

Singaporeans love to eat seafood and will travel a long way and in difficult circumstances to get it. At weekends tiny wooden shacks along the Johor coast and on the offshore islands fill up with busloads of people after their special dish, be it drunken prawns or chilli crab.

Shopping, the second most practised activity on the island, is also a major topic for discussion over the dinner table. Each mall has its area of excellence and new malls are visited by families much as a new tourist destination.

Whatever activities they engage in, Singaporeans are both proud of and able to laugh at their country and its peculiar ways.

⏶ *The popular Maxwell Food Centre*

Culture

With three ethnic groups, Singapore has an amazing wealth of culture to call on. Around 78 per cent of the population is Chinese, 14 per cent Malay and 7 per cent Indian. The old ways of each culture are dwindling a little as each generation becomes more Singaporean, but certain features remain.

Chinese opera can be found at fairly impromptu locations at most times of the year but especially during the month of the Hungry Ghosts (see page 12), and stages appear overnight in town centres and marketplaces. The opera is a strange combination of slapstick, singing music and melodrama, enacted in Cantonese or Hokkien, the dressing room being the back of a lorry and the stage a rickety set of planks. The make-up and costume, accompanying music and singing are unmissable.

Also to be found in shopping centres, usually around Chinese New Year (see page 11), are the city's lion dancers. Generally formed from martial arts groups, the team of lion dancers (usually two men to a lion) and their accompanying musicians perform acrobatic dances, with firecrackers and cymbal crashing to drive out the spirits of the old year.

Indian classical music and dance is strong in the city and can be seen performed in many of its temples during religious festivals. Malay culture is more homely and less public, but there are performances of Malay dance and music at Istana Kampong Glam (page 80).

For more contemporary culture, the Theatres on the Bay are the best place to look. Concerts of classical and modern music as well as drama, both local and imported, are shown there.

The Victoria Theatre (ⓐ 9 Empress Palace), the **Arts House** (ⓐ 1 Old Parliament Lane ⓣ 6332 6900) and **Suntec City** (ⓐ 1 Raffles Boulevard ⓣ 6337 2888) are also venues for cultural performances. Other arts venues include the **Drama Centre at the National Library** (ⓐ 3F National Library, 100 Victoria St ⓣ 6332 325), **Substation** (ⓐ 45 Armenian St ⓣ 6337 7800) and the **DBS Drama Centre** (ⓐ 20 Merbau Rd ⓣ 6733 8166).

🔺 *The Victoria Theatre hosts regular concerts*

The **Singapore Symphony Orchestra** (ⓦ www.sso.org.sg) offers regular performances of the classics and popular music, while the **Singapore Chinese Orchestra** (ⓦ www.sco.com.sg) and performance groups from the Nanyang Academy of Fine Arts also have regular offerings. Occasionally the **Kallang Theatre** (ⓐ 1 Stadium Walk ⓣ 6345 8488) or **Singapore Indoor Stadium** (ⓐ 2 Stadium Walk ⓣ 6344 2660) play host to major productions from abroad.

The **Singapore Art Museum** (ⓐ 71 Bras Basah Rd ⓣ 6332 3222), the **Science Centre** (see page 111) and the **Esplanade Tunnel** (from Empress Place to Esplanade Park and Esplanade Theatres) regularly feature art exhibitions, and there are tens of small private art galleries throughout the city such as **Sculpture Square** (ⓐ 155 Middle Rd ⓣ 6333 1055), **Singapore Tyler Print Institute** (ⓐ 41 Robertson Quay ⓣ 6336 3663) and the **Opera Gallery** (ⓐ 391 Orchard Rd ⓣ 6735 2618). Public art includes several pieces by Roy Lichtenstein (called Singapore Brushstrokes) along the Millennia Walk. May sees the annual Singapore Arts Festival (www.singaporeartsfest.com).

ⓞ *Singapore harbour and city at night*

Shopping

If shopping was an Olympic sport, Singapore would win the gold, silver and bronze every time. Shopping is a major pastime and entire families will cheerfully troop out to Orchard Road or one of the other shopping centres to make a whole day of it. They'll eat in one of the food halls, take in a movie and only come home when all possibilities have been exhausted.

For visitors the problem will be how to make room in your luggage for the beautiful things you can buy at relatively low prices.

Fashionistas should check out Singapore's designers as well as the usual suspects. Good places to look for local designers are Bugis Junction, Far East Plaza and An Siang Hill in Chinatown. Names to look out for are Francis Cheong, Madeleine Wong and her Posse label, and K Mi Huang.

Tailor-made suits are an interesting option, although if you're travelling on to Bangkok or Hong Kong you'll get better deals in those places. Sarongs and saris, silk, batik and other fabrics can be found in Arab Street or Serangoon Road.

Jewellery is abundant and outside of the big department stores its price is negotiable. Look out for good gold items and semi-precious stones, particularly jade.

Singapore excels in arts and crafts. Look in the fixed-price Lim's in Holland Village, then move on to bargaining in Chinatown and Arab Street. Basketry, wood carvings, Chinese pottery, embroidered silks, wedding baskets, tiffin carriers, cooking utensils and wooden craft items from Bali are all worth looking for.

Electronics can be found in Sim Lim Square and Sim Lim Tower in Bencoolen Street, cameras in Orchard Road and computers in the Funan Centre in North Bridge Road. Be aware of the price of the item at home and in the local department stores, check guarantees are international and watch your goods being packed. You don't want any nasty surprises when you get home.

The tourist board produces a free shopping guide, and don't forget that you can claim back the Goods and Services Tax (GST) for purchases over S$100 if the retailer displays a Global Refund Tax Free Shopping sign (ⓦ www.globalrefund.com).

ⓘ Most shops and department stores open daily from around 09.30/10.00–21.00/21.30.

⬤ *Beautiful pottery, in every size, to choose from*

Eating & drinking

Singaporeans are passionate about food and eat it at every opportunity, whether at plastic tables in hawker centres (see page 28) or in high class restaurants in posh hotels. In Singapore there is a place to eat for every budget, occasion and palate.

Japanese, Thai, European, Korean, Asian fusion, Californian – all the world's cuisines are represented here, but the real eating adventure is to go native and try the local food.

The Singaporean version of Cantonese cooking is characterised by quickly stir fried, bite-sized pieces of food served with a ready-made thickened sauce, often laced with chilli so that sweet and sour sauce takes on a third dimension of hot.

Next in popularity is Szech cooking – stir fried combinations with contrasting textures, sesame flavoured, with no accompanying sauce but often served with a giant chilli on the plate.

Chinese haute cuisine is Beijing-style food, blander and based on wheat noodles rather than rice. It's most commonly encountered in expensive restaurants.

PRICE RATING

Price ratings in this book are based on the average price of a three-course meal without drinks.

£ = up to S$25 **££** = S$25–S$75 **£££** = more than S$75

Malay food can be found at the hawker places at Geylang and around Arab Street. Typical Malay food is known as *nasi padang* – a plate of rice to which you add your choice from a selection of very spicy, often coconut- and lemon grass-flavoured, curries.

Indian restaurants are mostly inexpensive places serving small dollops of rice, flatbreads and curries on banana leaves (or, more commonly these days, on steel or polystyrene trays). Muslim Indian curry houses serve a wonderful snack called *roti prata* – a crispy pancake often filled with meat or vegetables

🔺 *A sample of typical Singapore cuisine*

HAWKER CENTRES

These places comprise several small kitchen stalls, each serving its own specialities. On arrival, grab a cleared table and park one of your company on it. This can be a cut-throat affair at busy times and, especially at Newton Circus, tables can be earmarked by one particular stall hoping for a big party of *gweilos* (literally 'white ghosts', a name given to foreigners) with no idea of the cost of their food.

Having established your base roam the stalls, picking whatever you like and giving your table number. The food appears as if by magic, everybody eats and each stallholder retrieves his or her plates. If you order Muslim food, keep those utensils separate.

Dishes to look out for are: satay served with peanut sauce; *laksa* (a glorious soup made with coconut-flavoured curry sauce, rice noodles, shellfish and other bits and pieces); *yong tau fu* (another soup dish with stuffed vegetables added); chicken rice (a lovely simple Hainanese dish); chilli crab (an adventure, as you rip the shreds of meat from the exoskeleton); *mee goreng* (an Indian-influenced fried noodle dish); *roti john* (a French roll dipped in beaten egg and minced lamb and fried); and *tahu goreng* (deep-fried beancurd, served with salad and peanut sauce).

(when it becomes a *murtabak*) and accompanied by a fiery curry sauce. For breakfast there are other pancakes or breads; *paratha* is worth seeking out in Serangoon Road or *masala dosa* (rice and gram flour pancakes filled with potatoes and served with coconut sauce).

The best fun, though, is to try Singaporean cuisine served in a hawker centre (see opposite).

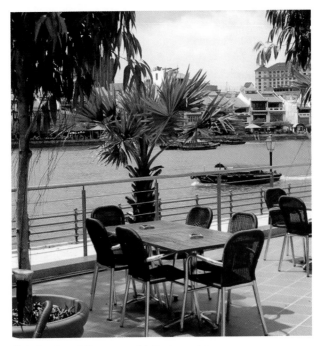

◆ *At Siem Reap Café you can watch the river go by*

Entertainment & nightlife

Singapore has a thriving nightlife centred around Boat and Clarke quays where the vast interiors of once crumbling and deserted *godowns* (warehouses) have been turned into huge clubs, bars and restaurants. The area has a dedicated comedy club, **1NiteStand** (ⓐ 3 River Valley Rd, Clarke Quay ① 6334 1954), which has nightly performances by local artists. If you want to catch some of the patterns of the local dialect, lovingly known as Singlish, this is the place to go.

Boat Quay, longer established as an entertainment centre, is possibly slightly wilder, but then this is Singapore we're talking about. Try wandering down Circular Road, just behind Boat Quay, where Bohemia in the form of Irish bars and occasional jazz performances have been known to occur.

🔺 *The Ministry of Sound in Clarke Quay*

A second area to check out is Mohamed Sultan Road, close to Robertson Quay where the newest bunch of night spots is emerging. Chijmes (see page 89) is a rather more sedate place where the entertainment continues till late. Karaoke is still as popular as ever in the city and there are karaoke bars in all the major hotspots.

 Alcohol is expensive and prices tend to go up as the venue gets classier. One way to avoid spending wads of cash is to imbibe during 'happy hours', when drinks are either half price or two for one.

 There is often a ladies' night midweek, when drinks or the admission charge are free for females.

Live music does quite well in Singapore. For the really big names **Singapore Indoor Stadium** (see page 22) comes into play. For jazz

AFTER HOURS
Bars tend to close between midnight and 01.00, and the clubs at around 03.00. At this point most Singaporeans head off for some food or an early breakfast. Hawker centres are the best for this. Newton and Lau Pa Sat in Shenton Way stay open 24 hours, as does the café in the Hyatt Hotel.
   During the summer there are performances of all kinds at Fort Canning Hill and other parks (www.nparks.gov.sg).

enthusiasts **Jazz@Southbridge** (@ 82b Boat Quay ① 6327 4671) is almost a Singaporean institution, as is **Harry's Bar** (@ 28 Boat Quay ① 6538 3029). The **Lobby Bar** at the Intercontinental (@ 80 Middle Rd ① 6338 7600) has a smoochy kind of jazz, while the **Crazy Elephant** (@ 3E River Valley Rd ① 6337 7859), among others at Clarke Quay, has a resident rock band, and **Rouge**, at Peranakan Place, offers live alternative rock.

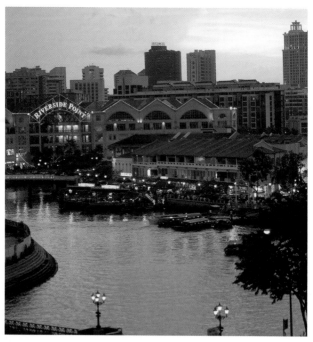

◆ *Clarke Quay, centre of Singaporean nightlife*

Going to the movies is a much appreciated form of entertainment in Singapore. Theatres show a range of films in different languages, from Cantonese and Malay to Tamil, all subtitled in English, and western, Hollywood films subtitled in all three languages, which can occasionally interfere with events on the screen.

Alliance Francaise Theatre (ⓐ 1 Sarkies Rd ❶ 6737 8422) shows weekly films in French, and the **British Council** (ⓐ 30 Napier Rd ❶ 6473 1111) has occasional offerings. For listings of what's on, check out the free monthly magazine *Where*, available from hotel lobbies, tourist offices and other public places. For advance ticket bookings contact either **SISTIC** (❶ 6348 5555 ⓦ www.sistic.com) or **Ticketcharge** (❶ 6296 2929 ⓦ www.ticketcharge.com.sg).

❶ Cinema seats are very cold, inexpensive and very popular, so you should bring an extra layer, get your tickets in advance and be there early. Be prepared for the locals chatting throughout the movie. Singaporeans also enjoy snacks while viewing, so expect the sound of popcorn crunching.

Sport & relaxation

With acres of water, an indecent number of golf courses and swimming pools, inexpensive squash courts, and miles of cycle and rollerblade-friendly paths, Singapore offers lots of opportunities for burning off all that hawker food.

Cricket
Singapore Cricket Club Entry to the club is members only but you can watch matches from the Padang (🕐 Sat pm & Sun am Mar–Oct).

Cycling
Bike & Hike 🅰 382 Upper Bukit Timah Rd 🕿 6763 8382
Comfort Rental 🅰 18 Pulau Ubin 🕿 6542 0557
🅦 www.avipclub.com.sg/comfort 🕐 08.00–18.00
Rental kiosk 🅐 East Coast Park by McDonald's 🕐 08.00–20.00 Sat, Sun & public holidays, 09.00–20.00 Mon–Fri

Football
Eleven teams play in the National Football League over the eight months of the football season. International games are played at the **National Stadium** (🅐 Kallang 🕐 09.00–17.00 Mon–Fri) from where tickets can be obtained.

Golf
Changi Golf Club 🅐 20 Netheravon Rd 🕿 6545 5133
Jurong Country Club 🅐 9 Science Centre Rd 🕿 6568 5188
Sentosa Gold Club 🅐 27 Bukit Manis Rd 🕿 6275 0022

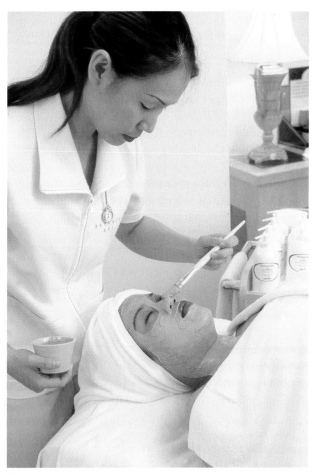

🔺 *Retreat to a spa for some real relaxation*

Horse racing
Singapore Turf Club ⓐ 1 Turf Club Ave ⓣ 6879 1000
ⓦ www.turfclub.com.sg

Reverse bungee jumping
GMax Reverse Bungee Jump ⓐ 3E River Valley Rd, Clarke Quay
ⓣ 6338 1146 ⓦ www.gmax.co.nz ⓛ 15.00–01.00 Mon–Thur,
15.00–03.00 Fri, 12.00–03.00 Sat, 12.00–01.00 Sun

Spas
The Retreat Spa & Thalasso Centre ⓐ Changi Village Hotel,
1 Netheravon Rd ⓣ 6738 0080 ⓦ www.theretreat.com.sg
Spa-lon ⓐ Chijmes ⓣ 6837 0131 ⓦ www.thespa-lon.com
Spa Valley ⓐ 02-02 Cairnhill Place ⓣ 6738 0889
ⓦ www.spavalley.com ⓛ 10.00–19.00

Swimming
Buona Vista Swimming Complex ⓐ 76 Holland Drive
River Valley Swimming Complex ⓐ River Valley Rd

Water skiing & wakeboarding
Kallang Riverside Park ⓣ 6344 8813 ⓦ www.extreme.com.sg
Proair Watersports ⓐ Punggol Marina 600, Punggol Avenue 17
ⓣ 6756 8012 ⓦ www.proairwatersports.com

Windsurfing
East Coast Sea Sports Club ⓐ 1390 East Coast Parkway
ⓛ 09.30–18.00 Wed–Sun ⓦ www.water-venture.org.sg

Accommodation

Singapore offers a wide range of places to stay, from the basic to the super-indulgent, according to your needs and your pocket. Little India and the Arab Street area are the centres for budget accommodation. Here you will find hostels with private single and double rooms as well as dorm beds. Both areas are good centres for socialising with fellow travellers and gathering information on the whole Asian travel scene.

The Inncrowd £ Backpacker's hostel in the heart of Little India with all the amenities you would expect. If full, try the Fragrance Backpackers Hostel (ⓦ www.fragrancebackpackers.com.sg) next door.
ⓐ 73 Dunlop St ⓣ 6296 6169 ⓦ www.the-inncrowd.com
Ⓜ MRT: Bugis or Little India

Sleepy Sam's £ Good location in a pedestrianised street near Arab Street, with mixed and female-only dorms, private single and double rooms, free Internet, kitchen and safe deposit.
ⓐ 55 Bussorah St ⓣ 9277 4988 ⓦ www.sleepysams.com
Ⓜ MRT: Bugis

PRICE RATING
The ratings in this book indicate the approximate cost of a room for two people for one night, including tax and breakfast.
£ = under S$75   ££ = S$75–S$200   £££ = over S$200

A Travellers Rest-Stop £ Dorm beds plus private en suite rooms with double and twin beds. Facilities include kitchen, laundry and bicycle rental. Chinatown location.
ⓐ 5 Teck Lim Rd, off Keong Saik Rd ☎ 6225 4812
ⓦ www.atravellersreststop.com.sg ⓝ MRT: Outram Park

hangout@mt.emily ££ Hip and affordable with deckchairs on the rooftop, washing machines and dryers, baggage storage, free broadband, private en suite bedrooms and shared rooms, plus air-conditioning. Good deal all round. ⓐ 10A Upper Wilkie Rd ☎ 6438 5588 ⓦ www.hangouthotels.com ⓝ MRT: Little India

Hotel 1929 ££ A good mid-range hotel in the heart of Chinatown. ⓐ 50 Keong Saik Rd ☎ 6347 1929
ⓦ www.hotel1929.com ⓝ MRT: Chinatown

Perak Hotel ££ A 35-room hotel close to Little India occupying a restored Chinese shop-house; fridge and tea/coffee maker in rooms. ⓐ 12 Perak Rd ☎ 6299 7733 ⓦ www.peraklodge.net
ⓝ MRT: Bugis or Little India

HOTEL 81s

Dotted around Singapore are a group of hotels called Hotel 81. These offer the best deals in terms of quality budget accommodation. Prices vary according to location, which includes central areas like Chinatown and Bugis, and to the type of bedroom. Well worth checking out the website ⓦ www.hotel81.com.sg

Swissôtel Merchant Court ££ More than 475 comfortable rooms, good food and beverage outlets and an in-house spa. Conveniently located for the city centre and Chinatown. ⓐ 20 Merchant Rd ⓣ 6337 2288 ⓦ singapore-merchantcourt.swissotel.com ⓝ MRT: Clarke Court

⬥ *The modern and arty lobby of the New Majestic*

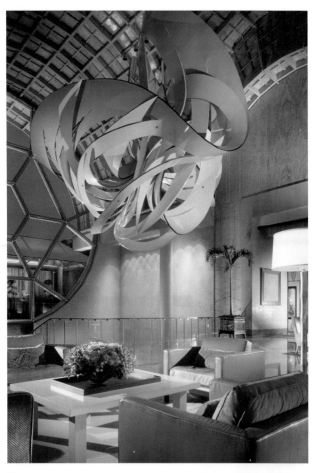

● *Luxury at The Ritz-Carlton Millenia*

New Majestic £££ Each of the 30 rooms is individually designed, hence a variety of price categories, but expect something bold and arty. There's a good Cantonese restaurant on the premises. ⓐ 31 Bukit Pasah Rd ⓣ 6222 3377 ⓦ www.newmajestichotel.com ⓝ MRT: Chinatown

The Ritz-Carlton Millenia £££ For pampering, attentive service and sheer indulgence of the senses, no hotel in Singapore is equal to The Ritz-Carlton. The public artwork is outstanding. ⓦ 7 Raffles Avenue ⓣ 6337 8888 ⓦ www.ritzcarlton.com ⓝ MRT: City Hall

The Scarlet £££ In Chinatown, this boutique hotel has sex appeal as well as two good restaurants, a relaxing bar, a gym and an outdoor Jacuzzi. ⓐ 33 Erskine Rd ⓣ 6511 3333 ⓦ www.thescarlethotel.com ⓝ MRT: Chinatown

THE BEST OF SINGAPORE

Singapore may well be the perfect holiday destination. You need at least a long weekend here and could easily fill a fortnight. There's shopping, eating, enjoying nature, all the fun of the fair at Sentosa, a bit of culture at the Esplanade, lots of history, ethnic diversity and a bit more shopping ...

TOP 10 ATTRACTIONS

- **Boat Quay** Enjoy the lights and food at night (see page 90).

- **Bukit Timah Nature Reserve** Encounter nature in the raw (see page 117).

- **Chinatown** Wonder at the food and medicine stalls, and finish with an authentic Chinese meal (see page 90).

- **Pulau Ubin** Take a bumboat, and enjoy Kampong life and a cycle ride (see page 119).

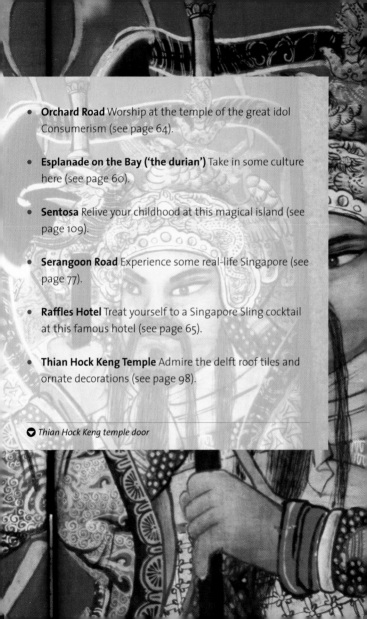

- **Orchard Road** Worship at the temple of the great idol Consumerism (see page 64).

- **Esplanade on the Bay ('the durian')** Take in some culture here (see page 60).

- **Sentosa** Relive your childhood at this magical island (see page 109).

- **Serangoon Road** Experience some real-life Singapore (see page 77).

- **Raffles Hotel** Treat yourself to a Singapore Sling cocktail at this famous hotel (see page 65).

- **Thian Hock Keng Temple** Admire the delft roof tiles and ornate decorations (see page 98).

▼ *Thian Hock Keng temple door*

HALF-DAY: SINGAPORE IN A HURRY

With just half a day, Orchard Road is the place for you. It sums up what Singapore is all about and contains some of its most in-your-face architecture. Start off at Orchard MRT station, enjoy the wonders of Tang's with its comfortable floors of everything you ever wanted, then move on through Lucky Plaza where you can see cut-throat selling at work. Work your way down to the newly reopened National Museum in Stamford Road and catch the exhibitions on food and shopping there as well as some history. Try to make time for Raffles, where you can enjoy a Singapore Sling.

1 DAY: TIME TO SEE A LITTLE MORE

In a day you can take in Fort Canning Hill and the Battle Box. Wander round to the Asian Civilisations Museum and then you can end up in the evening at Boat Quay enjoying the brou-ha-ha of Singaporeans letting it all hang out. If you have a mind, head into Zouk (page 102).

2–3 DAYS: SHORT CITY BREAK

Spend one early morning in the Botanic Gardens and the orchid garden, but also look out for groups of people practising tai chi. In the afternoon make your way to Chinatown for more shopping. Take in the Thian Hock Keng Temple and check out the wetmarket, where some unusual things are waiting to become someone's dinner. Stay in Chinatown for the evening, where the night market in Smith Street offers lots of Chinese delicacies for your evening meal. Another early start could bring you to Singapore Zoo, where you can enjoy breakfast with the animals. For lunch head back to Bukit Timah, where you can pick up a picnic lunch and head off to Bukit Timah Hill – a wonderful relic of what Singapore was like before civilisation hit it. In the evening Serangoon Road beckons, its shops and restaurants booming with Indian music and the temples alive with activity. Try a banana leaf dinner at one of the many restaurants.

LONGER: ENJOYING SINGAPORE TO THE FULL

With longer there is time for a whole day at Sentosa, another day out at Changi and on to Pulau Ubin, a trip out to Jurong and some shopping around Arab Street. Your evenings can be split between the Esplanade on the Bay, Boat Quay and some of the lively hawker centres such as Lau Pa Sat, Maxwell Street or Newton Circus.

⬥ *Boat Quay at night*

Something for nothing

Just the expression 'something for nothing' would put many of Singapore's merchants into a state of apoplexy. That said, there are things to do here that won't cost you a cent.

Clearly, window shopping has to be the most entertaining activity and has the advantage of being largely inside so there is the added blessing of free air-conditioning.

There are hours of fun to be had at the **Botanic Gardens** (see page 105) and at **Fort Canning Hill** (see page 60) (including several free performances through the summer months), while

⬤ *Wander around Bukit Timah Nature Reserve for free on weekdays*

When it rains

When it rains in Singapore there is absolutely nothing to be done outside. Singaporean rain is scary in its intensity: vision is reduced to a few feet, storm drains fill and roar in a matter of minutes, and everyone runs for the nearest shelter – preferably

⬥ *When it rains, try a spot of indoor shopping*

not a tree on account of the accompanying lightening. Bridges over the motorway fill up with moped riders sheltering from the deluge, and shopping centres fill even fuller. The good news is that most downpours last only 30 minutes or so and the resulting coolness is worth the wait.

If you experience one of the few days when the rain just won't go away there are the museums you can visit: the Battlebox, the National Museum, the Asian Civilisations Museum and Raffles Museum (with the added advantage of Singapore Slings while you wait to go out again).

The shopping malls along Orchard Road, linked with a few dashes in the open, could take a week to seriously explore. Along some of the older shopping streets, such as Arab Street, the covered footpaths (known as 'five foot ways') offer a dry route from shop to shop.

The cinema is a joy in Singapore. You could try a Cantonese movie subtitled in English, or even a Hindi or Malay movie with their abrupt shifts from violence to song and dance.

One of Singapore's covered wetmarkets is an education in food tastes and can offer a good 30 minutes of fascinating study of the things that people consider food. Most wetmarkets have hawker centres attached where you can try some local delicacies.

Considering the briefness of Singapore's showers and the fact that most of them seem to start around lunchtime, an hour in a restaurant is also an enjoyable occupation. Or, you can find shelter outside – such as the five foot ways or a shop doorway – just watching the vast amounts of water falling out of the sky can be quite entertaining, too.

On arrival

ARRIVING

By air

You cannot fail to be impressed by Changi Airport, which is like a little city and could survive entirely on its own even if all the rest of the island disappeared. Facilities at the airport include shopping centres, hotels, free sleeping areas, showers, a free trip around town for transit passengers, cinemas, wireless Internet connection, games areas, several food courts, post offices, money exchange, banks and left luggage.

The airport is linked to the city centre by MRT, bus and several taxi options, as well as a city shuttle.

The MRT links terminal 2 with the city. Fares are S$1.50 and the journey takes 40 minutes or so. An alternative is to take a

🔺 *The bus system in Singapore is well run*

maxicab; these leave every 15 minutes and will take you, along with other passengers, to your hotel. The most expensive option is a regular taxi, which will cost around S$20.

By rail
Trains from Malaysia and Thailand arrive at Keppel Street train station, where you will encounter passport control and some sniffer dogs. A cab or bus 97 will bring you into town. Cabs are metered.

By bus
Buses from Malaysia and Thailand come directly into the city to Lavender Road Coach Terminal or the Jahore Bahru Bus Depot on Queen Street, depending on the bus company. Both terminals are in the city centre and close to MRT stations.

Driving in Singapore
There really is very little reason to drive in Singapore. Parking is expensive and tolls are levied every time you enter the restricted areas during business hours. Add to this traffic jams and a surcharge for travelling into Malaysia, and the thought of the traffic-free MRT sounds better every minute.

TIME DIFFERENCES
Singapore is 8 hours ahead of London (GMT), 13 hours ahead of New York and Toronto (Eastern Standard Time), 14 hours ahead of Chicago, 16 hours ahead of San Francisco and Vancouver, and 2 hours behind Sydney, 5 behind Wellington and 6 hours ahead of Johannesburg.

Singapore city

Symbol	Legend
Ⓜ	MRT Stop
✝	Cathedral
𝑖	Information
✈	Airport
▭	Railway Stn
▭	Bus Station
✚	Hospital

0 — 600 metres
0 — 600 yards

FINDING YOUR FEET

The first bit of acclimatising is to slow down! The place is seriously hot so energetic walking will exhaust you. Singaporeans know their way around town via air-conditioned routes, shady pathways and the MRT, and the wise tourist will follow their example. Once you have learned to spot a good bit of shade and bought an umbrella (twofold usage: shade in desperation and keeping off the rain while you run for shelter), it's time to realise that this is a fine country. There are fines for most things you take for granted – especially jaywalking, snacking on the MRT and chewing on gum.

Traffic, like everything else in Singapore, obeys the rules, so no speeding cars but also no slowing down for wandering pedestrians. Crime is not a big issue in the city, but it is as well to follow the rules of any big city – avoid parks alone late at night, keep your belongings safe in your hotel room and be aware of where your handbag/wallet is at all times. Pickpockets operate in crowded areas and especially love backpacks and people with buggies – they are easy to distract. You must remember to drink more (water!) and use sunscreen.

ORIENTATION

Singapore is a tiny city state. Most of the sights, hotels, restaurants and shopping centres are located close together, which is fortunate since the heat can be overpowering.

The river forms the heart of the city, flowing roughly east–west across the island, with both of its banks filled with bars, clubs and restaurants, replacing the old commercial port of Singapore. To the north and running vaguely parallel is Orchard

Road and between them lies the financial district. North again is Little India and the Arab Quarter. Immediately south of the river is Chinatown.

Beyond these central areas lay satellite towns. To the east is Changi and the tiny island of Pulau Ubin; to the far west is Jurong with the Bird Park and Sentosa; and to the north, Sungei Buloh and the wild lands of Woodlands and Johor Bahru.

If you get lost, everyone speaks English (or anyway, Singlish) and will be pleased to put you right.

ⓘ The tourist board hands out maps of the island, which will be all you need to navigate your way around.

GETTING AROUND

Considerable thought has to be given to getting around Singapore. Just 10 minutes' walk can make children ratty and ruin a linen outfit.

Public transport

The MRT is a godsend. Its three lines – north–south, north–east and east–west – cover most tourist destinations. Trains run from 05.30–00.30 and fares begin at 90 cents. Single fares can be bought at machines in each station or you can buy an ez-link card, which (like the British Oyster card) is rechargeable and valid on buses too. For a S$5 refundable deposit you can buy a card in MRT stations with a minimum value of S$10, which is convenient and makes journeys slightly cheaper. Do not eat or drink, smoke or carry *durians* (a popular fruit) on the MRT.

The bus network covers the entire island and if you are a bus enthusiast you can make every journey that way. Fares start at

Johor

Selat Johor

Kuala Lumpur

Admiralty   Sembawang

Woodlands

Marsling

Kranji

Lim Chu Kang

Yew Tee

Choa Chu Kang

Yishun

Khatib

(138)
Singapore Zoological
Gardens Terminal

Choa Chu Kang

Bukit Gombak

Bukit Batok

(156) (410)
Macritchie
Reservoir

(2)
Boon Lay

Chinese
Garden

Lakeside

(4)
Jurong East

Toa Payoh

(67)

Novena

(182)
(251)

(335)

(154)

Clementi

Bukit Panjang

Newton

Orchard

(200)
Kent Ridge

Dover

Buona Vista

Commonwealth

Pasir
Panjang

Selat Jurong

Queenstown

Redhill

Tiong Bahru   Chinatown

SMRT (Singapore Mass Rapid Transit)
East West Line
North East Line
North South Line
Circle Line

LRT (Light Rapid Transit)
Sengkang East (Inner & Outer)
Sengkang West (Inner & Outer)

Selected connecting bus routes

Featured ferry route

KTMB (Keretapi Tanah Melayu Berhad)
Inter-City service

Outram
Park

(6) HarbourFront

(Bedok)   Route terminus station

(1)   Destination or Route Number

∞   Interchange

(6) HarbourFront   Tanjong
                       Pagar

Sentosa

90 cents and you must have the exact fare. You can use the ez-link card on buses. Some buses are not air-conditioned.

❶ There are several tourist-orientated buses running from one sight to another. The SIA hop-on hop-off bus runs from Orchard Road, Suntec City, Clarke Quay and Marina Bay. Another route travels to Sentosa. You can buy a day pass for S$12. Alternatively, if you are an SIA traveller use of the buses is free.

Taxis

Compared to Europe these are inexpensive and abundant – and also another method of heat avoidance. They are metered, so you don't have to worry about negotiating fares, and many of them have credit card machines. Fares start at S$2.40, and there are extra charges for use of the boot, journeys after midnight, booking in advance, passing into the Electronic Road Pricing (ERP) area and pick up from the airport. If your taxi starts to 'bing' at regular intervals, the driver is speeding. Cabs have a built-in speed limit monitor.

Car hire

If you need to hire a car, you are required to show proof of identification and your driving licence. You must also buy a stored value cash card to drive into the ERP area and parking coupons which can be bought at booths close to car parks and 7–Eleven stores.

Avis Terminal ⓐ 2 Changi Airport ❶ 6542 8855
Hertz Terminal ⓐ 2 Changi Airport ❶ 6542 5300

▶ *Singapore's biggest mosque – Sultan Mosque*

Orchard Road & Colonial District

The historical, emotional and cultural heart of the city, this area is where you will spend most of your time when it comes to shopping, exploring museums and finding good places to eat.

SIGHTS & ATTRACTIONS

Esplanade – Theatres on the Bay
Nicknamed by locals 'the durian' on account of the complex's spiky appearance, this gobsmacking site occupies 6 hectares (15 acres) of reclaimed land and includes a concert hall, theatre, two performance studios, two outdoor theatre spaces, lots of – surprise! – F&B (food and beverage) outlets and a shopping mall.

🅰 1 Esplanade Drive ☎ 6828 8377 (general); 6348 555 (tickets) 🅦 www.esplanade.com 🕐 10.00–22.00; free guided tours 11.00 & 14.00 Mon–Fri Ⓝ MRT: City Hall; Bus: 36, 56, 75, 77, 97, 106, 111, 133, 162, 171, 174M, 195, 700A. Admission charge for theatre performances

Fort Canning Park
Somehow, amid this concrete jungle of a city, this little park has survived. Right behind the commercial hubbub of Orchard Road, orioles sing, cicadas chirrup and all manner of unregulated creatures lurk. The 19th-century gravestones of the early white folk have been relocated to the park walls, the crumbling army buildings given a new lease of life in the form of an arts and cooking (what else?) academy, and F&B outlets

and Raffles' botanic garden and lighthouse have been born again.
🅐 Fort Canning Hill, entrances at Hill St, Canning Rise, Percival
Rd, River Valley Rd, Canning Walk ☎ 6332 1200
🅦 www.nparks.gov.sg Ⓜ MRT: Dhoby Ghaut; Bus to Penang Rd: 7,
14, 16, 36, 64, 65, 77, 106, 111, 124, 162, 167, 171, 174

Raffles' Landing Site
The place where it is thought that Sir Stamford Raffles,
Singapore's founder, might have stepped ashore in 1819 is
marked with a marble statue of the man himself. Nice river

🔵 *Esplanade – Theatres on the Bay – is on the waterfront overlooking Marine Bay*

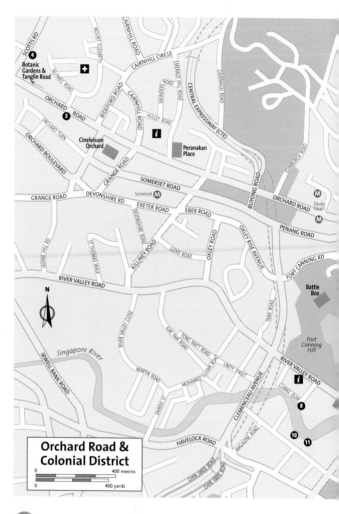

Orchard Road & Colonial District

scenes, and close by are all the delights of Boat Quay and the Asian Civilisations Museum.

ⓐ Boat Quay Ⓜ MRT: Raffles Place; Bus: 70, 82, 97, 100, 107, 130, 131, 162, 167, 196, 700

Orchard Road

Possibly the world's most densely packed shopping street, Orchard Road is a mile of consumerism deified. While once-great architects built huge edifices in praise of an omnipresent, omnipotent and divine being, in this street all that genius, beauty, glass and granite has gone into retail. Look on their works ye mighty and despair.

ⓐ Orchard Rd Ⓜ MRT: Orchard, Somerset

The Padang

The place where once crinolined ladies with powdered hair took their evening stroll, the Padang has been a sport and recreation area since Raffles decided it would be in the early 19th century. In the southeast corner is the Singapore Cricket Club, established for the exclusive use of white men and still very exclusive, while on the other side is the Singapore Recreation Club, set up by the *stengahs*, Singapore's 19th-century mixed race community.

THE SINGAPORE FLYER

Singapore's latest addition to its compelling set of reasons to visit is this bigger, better and classier version of the London Eye, located at the south-east tip of the Marina Centre, but still under construction at the time of writing.

Raffles Hotel

For years in the 20th century a run-down, sleazy kind of place, in 1991 it got the Singapore treatment and is the glossy institution you see before you. The building became an exclusive hotel in the 1880s. A-list celebs started staying here long before Michael Jackson graced its luxury suite – Joseph Conrad, Somerset Maugham, Noel Coward, Rudyard Kipling and many more. The lobby is open to non-paying guests – no riff-raff though. If you don't look well dressed enough you may be asked to leave.

ⓐ 1 Beach Rd ⓣ 6412 1143 ⓦ www.raffles.com ⓝ MRT: City Hall; Bus: 7, 14, 16, 36, 77, 97, 131, 162, 167, 171, 700

CULTURE

Asian Civilisations Museum

The ten or so galleries cover Asian cultural life from Islam to China and all stops in between. The best bit is the gallery dedicated to the life of the Singapore River, its banks now a glitzy series of outlets but once the economic heart of the island. A second branch in the restored Tao Nan School in Armenian Street focuses on Chinese and Peranakan culture.

ⓐ 1 Empress Place ⓣ 6332 7798 ⓦ www.museum.org.sg
ⓛ 09.00–19.00 Tues–Thur, Sat & Sun, 13.00–19.00 Mon, 09.00–21.00 Fri ⓝ MRT: Raffles Place; Bus: 70, 82, 97, 100, 107, 130, 131, 162, 167, 196, 700. Admission charge (covers both branches)
ⓐ 39 Armenian St ⓣ 6332 3015 ⓦ www.museum.org.sg
ⓛ 09.00–19.00 Tues–Thur, Sat & Sun, 13.00–19.00 Mon, 09.00–21.00 Fri ⓝ MRT: City Hall; Bus: 7, 14, 16, 36, 77, 97, 131, 162, 167, 171, 700. Admission charge (covers both museums)

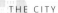
Battle Box

This series of underground bunkers was the headquarters of the British command during World War II. It was from here that the British decided to surrender to the Japanese. The 26 chambers contain authentic machinery and other items used, and gives a very stark impression of what life must have been like for those cramped in down here with not enough air and the sound of bombs falling overhead.

⬥ *The National Museum of Singapore is an impressive building*

ⓐ 51 Canning Rise ❶ 6333 0510 ⏱ 10.00–18.00, closed 1st day of Chinese New Year Ⓝ MRT: Dhoby Ghaut; Bus to Penang Rd: 7, 14, 16, 36, 64, 65, 77, 106, 111, 124, 162, 167, 171, 174. Admission charge

National Museum of Singapore
Newly reopened after three years of renovations, the museum and its new extension offer a history of the island, exhibitions of contemporary life and much more.
ⓐ 93 Stamford Rd ❶ 6332 3659 ⓦ www.nationalmuseum.sg
⏱ History Gallery: 10.00–18.00; Living Galleries: 10.00–21.00
Ⓝ MRT: Dhoby Ghaut. Admission charge

Raffles Hotel Museum
Full of bits and pieces turned up by locals, such as old photos and maps, plus memorabilia that survived the wilderness years after World War II, the museum is well worth a few minutes' nostalgia for an almost forgotten way of life.
ⓐ 1 Beach Rd ❶ 6412 1143 ⓦ www.raffles.com ⏱ 10.00–19.00
Ⓝ MRT: City Hall; Bus: 7, 14, 16, 36, 77, 97, 131, 162, 167, 171, 700

RETAIL THERAPY

Asian Civilisations Museum Shop Offering quality arts and crafts, museum replicas, fixed prices and a calm atmosphere; the shop can be visited without having to pay to visit the museum. ⓐ 1 Empress Place ❶ 6332 7798
ⓦ www.museumshop.com.sg ⏱ 09.00–19.00 Tues–Thur, Sat & Sun, 13.00–19.00 Mon, 09.00–21.00 Fri Ⓝ MRT: City Hall, Raffles Place; Bus: 70, 82, 97, 100, 107, 130, 131, 162, 167, 196, 700

Chapter 2 Hairdressing salon with a reputation for quality cuts but, although the basic deals are reasonably priced, expect to pay a lot for anything special. ⓐ 03-258 Marina Square, 6 Raffles Boulevard ⓣ 6338 0112 ⓦ www.chapter-2.com ⓛ 11.00–22.00 ⓜ MRT: City Hall

Marina Square Shopping Mall Linked to the Marina Mandarin, The Oriental and Pan Pacific hotels, this is a premier shopping mall where bargains are rare. Mostly fashion and lifestyle outlets. ⓐ Marina Bay ⓦ www.marinasquare.com.sg ⓛ 10.00–22.00 ⓜ MRT: City Hall (an extension of the MRT line to Marina Square might be operational by the time you read this)

Orchard Road: Scotts Road to Plaza Singapura The junction of Orchard Road and Scotts Road is dominated by **Tangs**, one of the best all-purpose department stores in the city, while on Scotts Road itself **Far East Plaza** is good for avant-garde fashions from overseas. **Lucky Plaza**, next to Tangs, has camera and electronics shops but could prove unlucky if you don't already have an idea of a product's price. **Wisma Atria**, across the road, has affordable fashion and lifestyle outlets (and an inexpensive food hall). Next door, the huge and monstrous-looking **Ngee Ann City** has a large bookstore and countless shops. Further up the road, **Specialists** has a good department store and middle-of-the-road retail shops. Opposite, Centrepoint has the reputable **Robinsons** department store and a myriad of assorted shops. **Plaza Singapura** has a bit of everything and avoids being outrageously expensive. ⓐ Orchard Rd from Scotts Rd junction to Plaza Singapura ⓦ www.fareast-plaza.com, www.centrepoint.com.sg,

www.ngeeanncity.com.sg, www.wismaonline.com
🕐 10.00–22.00 Ⓝ MRT: Somerset, Dhoby Ghaut

Orchard Road: Tanglin to Scotts Road Tanglin Road, which runs into the bottom end of Orchard Road, has three shopping malls – **Tanglin**, **Tudor Court** and **Tanglin Place** – full of artwork and antique outlets. **The Forum**, further up on Orchard Road itself, is good for toys and children's clothes. **Hilton Shopping Centre**, next door, is rather haute couture but for more affordable fashions walk up to Liat Towers and Wheelock Place.
ⓐ Tanglin Rd & Orchard Rd up to Scotts Rd 🕐 10.00–22.00
Ⓝ MRT: Orchard

Planet Traveller Everything for the traveller by way of luggage, accessories and assorted gadgets, plus a useful repair service (closed on Sun) for jammed locks, ripped zips and such like.
ⓐ 03-113 Marina Square Shopping Mall ☏ 6337 0291
ⓦ www.planettraveller.com 🕐 11.00–1900 Ⓝ MRT: City Hall

Raffles Shop Just about everything here has the Raffles logo, from key rings to a S$999 crystal tiger. The items that shift most quickly off the shelves are Singapore Sling glasses. ⓐ 1 Beach Rd
☏ 6412 1143 🕐 08.30–21.00 Ⓝ MRT: City Hall; Bus: 7, 14, 16, 36, 77, 97, 131, 162, 167, 171, 700

Royal Selangor Hundreds of pewter items suitable as gifts or for your own home. Factory tours also available; café in the shop.
ⓐ Clarke Quay ☏ 6268 9600 🕐 09.00–21.00 Ⓝ MRT: Clarke Quay; Bus: 54 (from Scotts Rd), 32, 195 (from City Hall MRT station)

Suntec City Mall From City Hall MRT station, you run a gauntlet of consumer outlets in the subterranean City Link Mall to reach Suntec City where more than 1,000 retail stores make this the largest shopping mall in Singapore. There is little use coming here without a healthy set of credit cards but, for the super solvent, this is a consumer's paradise. ☎ 6268 9600 🌐 www.suntecity.com.sg 🕐 09.00–22.00 Ⓜ MRT: City Hall (Exit G, via CityLink Mall)

TAKING A BREAK

Chocz £ ❶ Chocolate fondues, muffins, apple crumble, cakes galore, milk shakes, sodas and coffees. 🅐 02-15 Esplanade Mall ☎ 6238 0803 🌐 www.chocz.com.sg 🕐 11.00–21.00 Ⓜ MRT: City Hall

Food Republic £ ❷ Probably the best food centre along Orchard Road, come here for Indian, Thai or Chinese. Very busy at lunchtime so get your drink first and leave it on a table to reserve a seat while collecting your food. 🅐 4th Level, Wisma Atria, Orchard Rd 🕐 09.00–21.00 Ⓜ MRT: Orchard

Marina Food Loft £ ❸ Sit inside for air-conditioned comfort or outside in the evening under fans and facing the river. Great outlets here, like Thai Delights, Sammy's Curry Restaurant, Buona Pasta and Claypot Rice. 🅐 4th Level, Marina Square 🕐 11.00–22.00 Ⓜ MRT: City Hall

Picnic Food Court £ ❹ Mostly Chinese food outlets but also
Pastamania and Lerk Thai and, ideal for vegetarians, filling
yogurts at Yami. ⓐ Basement Level, Scotts Shopping Centre,
Scotts Rd 🕒 11.00–22.00 Ⓜ MRT: Orchard

Siem Reap II Café £ ❺ Salads, Western and Asian food, desserts
and children's menu. Sit outside facing the river with a cold beer
or iced coffee. ⓐ Asian Civilisations Museum, 1 Empress Place
❶ 6338 7596 Ⓦ www.indochine.com.sg 🕒 11.00–22.30
Ⓜ MRT: Raffles Place; Bus: 70, 82, 97, 100, 107, 130, 131, 162, 167, 196, 700

Singapore Art Café £ ❻ Next to the library, this is a bright and
airy place for a coffee, salad, vegetarian or pasta meals. ⓐ 03-02
Esplanade Mall, 8 Raffles Avenue ❶ 6336 4427
Ⓦ www.singaporeartcafe.com 🕒 12.00–21.00 Mon–Sat,

> **THE LEGENDARY LONG BAR**
> The Long Bar at the Raffles Hotel has been a popular
> drinking hole since the hotel opened in 1887. If you go
> there now the only drink you are likely to see being served
> is the famous, but not exactly addictive, Singapore Sling.
> This famous cocktail was created by bartender Ngiam
> Tong Boon in 1915 and an average of 2,000, at S$20 a shot,
> are sold every day in the hotel's various outlets.
> ⓐ Raffles Hotel, 1 Beach Rd ❶ 6412 1229 🕒 11.00–00.30
> Sun–Thur, 11.00–23.30 Fri & Sat; happy hour 17.00–21.00
> Sun–Thur Ⓜ MRT: City Hall; Bus: 7, 14, 16, 36, 77, 97, 131, 162,
> 167, 171 ,700

13.00–21.00 Sun Ⓝ MRT: City Hall; Bus: 36, 56, 75, 77, 97, 106, 111, 133, 162, 171, 174M, 195, 700A

AFTER DARK

Restaurants

Greenhouse ££ ❼ Never mind the Sunday Champagne brunch, Greenhouse undoubtedly offers the best evening buffet in the city, and on Friday and Saturday nights gourmets meet gourmands at a seafood feast. ⓐ Ritz-Carlton Millenia, Raffles Avenue ❶ 6434 5288 ⓦ www.ritzcarlton.com ❶ 11.30–15.30, 18.30–22.30 Ⓝ MRT: City Hall

Madame Butterfly ££ ❽ The menu of southeast Asian dishes can be mixed with the one downstairs from Bar Cocoon (where the fried rice is superior). Check out the arctic-cold vodka cocktail bar. ⓐ Merchant's Court, Clarke Quay ❶ 6557 6266 ⓦ www.indochine.com.sg ❶ 19.00–23.00 Ⓝ MRT: Clarke Quay; Bus: 54 (from Scotts Rd), 32, 195 (from City Hall MRT station)

My Humble House ££ ❾ Convenient for a meal after a show, with Asian fusion dishes like *laksa* with rock oysters. ⓐ 02-27 Esplanade Mall, 8 Raffles Avenue ❶ 6423 1881 ⓦ www.tunglok.com ❶ 12.00–15.00, 18.30–23.00 Ⓝ MRT: City Hall; Bus: 36, 56, 75, 77, 97, 106, 111, 133, 162, 171, 174M, 195, 700A

Peony-Jade ££ ❿ Szechuan and Cantonese cuisine in an attractive, plush restaurant occupying a converted *godown*. Start with the soft shell crab or the hot and sour soup served in

◉ *Enjoying an evening buffet at Greenhouse*

a Martini glass, before tucking into the smoked duck, or baked lamb or beef in a beer sauce. Block 3A, Clarke Quay 6338 0305 www.peony-jade.com 11.00–15.00, 18.00–23.00 MRT: Clarke Quay; Bus: 54 (from Scotts Rd), 32, 195 (from City Hall MRT station)

Quayside Seafood ££ Fresh seafood, including live lobster and prawns, and a choice of cooking methods. Reserve a riverside table for the best views. Clarke Quay 6338 0138 www.quaysideseafood.com 18.00–24.00 Sun–Thur, 18.00–01.00 Fri & Sat MRT: Clarke Quay; Bus: 54 (from Scotts Rd), 32, 195 (from City Hall MRT station)

Ristorante Bologna £££ Still *the* Italian restaurant in Singapore. Try the parma ham or porcini mushrooms with lobster for starters, while the pappadrelle with prawns and saffron sauce competes with fish, lamb and beef dishes as the best choice for main courses. Reserve a table by the window for the sound and sight of a waterfall. Sunday brunch is a feast. Marina Mandarin Hotel, Raffles Boulevard, Marina Square 6845 1111 www.marina-mandarin.com.sg 12.00–14.30 Mon–Fri, 18.30–22.30 Mon–Sat, 12.00–16.00 Sun MRT: City Hall

Bars

New Asia Bar This is the highest bar in Singapore, on the 71st floor of the Swissôtel. Stunning views of the city and on a clear night you can see the lights of Malaysia. Not the cheapest drinks in town but certainly the highest. Swissôtel, The

Stamford, 2 Stamford Rd ☎ 6431 7095 🕒 11.00–24.30 Sun–Thur, 11.00–23.30 Fri & Sat Ⓝ MRT: City Hall

Cinemas, theatres & shows

Cineleisure Orchard As well as the cinema complex, there is the e-gaming attraction E2Max@Cine–L9 with more than 160 e-gaming stations. Ⓐ 8 Grange Rd ☎ 6733 5969 ⓦ www.cathaycineleisure.com.sg 🕒 10.00–22.00 Ⓝ MRT: Somerset

Crazy Horse Paris This is as naughty as official Singapore gets – an 'artistic nude show', with a restaurant and nightclub to boot. Ⓐ 01-01 Clarke Quay ☎ 6336 1800 🕒 20.00 & 22.15 Tues–Sun, closed Mon, additional show at 24.00 Sat Ⓝ MRT: Clarke Quay; Bus: 54 (from Scotts Rd), 32, 195 (from City Hall MRT station)

Esplanade – Theatres on the Bay Asian and Western theatre, opera, musicals and dance and, every Friday to Sunday night, free outdoor performances. Ⓐ 1 Esplanade Drive ☎ 6828 8377 ⓦ www.esplanade.com 🕒 10.00–22.00 Ⓝ MRT: City Hall

Golden Village Multiscreen cinema complex with a bowling alley next door and snooker tables opposite. Ⓐ 3rd Level Marina Square ☎ 6334 3766 (cinema) ⓦ www.gv.com.sg (cinema, book online) 🕒 10.00–03.00 (bowling alley) Ⓝ MRT: City Hall

Little India & Arab Street

It is probably in this area of Singapore that visitors will come close to an idea of what the tiny city state was like for most of its existence. Serangoon Road especially is about as messy as Singapore gets with its traffic-clogged road, loud temples and small merchants selling traditional Indian goods. The Arab Street area has succumbed a little more to the renovators but still gives a sense of what things used to be like. Wheras most of the city's young people aspire to a condo, credit card and car this area is home to people and sights that are not encompassed by the new Singapore values.

Indians, many of them transported convicts from the British Empire, came to settle in this area around the middle of the 19th century when it contained brick kilns and herds of buffalo (hence some of the street names) and have stayed, with every new wave of immigrants heading for the area.

SIGHTS & ATTRACTIONS

Arab Street

By the time the state got round to renovating Arab Street the developers had learned their lesson and interfered as little as they could with the thriving community while ensuring that it provided maximum tourist interest. Arab Street, like it always has been, is a glorious blaze of colour – fabric shops, perfume shops, basketry, leather goods – perhaps more orientated to the tourist trade than 20 years ago but still occupied by one of Singapore's ethnic minorities. Great for shopping. ❷ Arab St

Little India Conservation Area

Perhaps a little less successful than its neighbouring conservation area, the Little India Conservation Area brings together the best of Indian culture in a tidy kind of way, although there's no substitute for a wander down Serangoon Road on a Sunday night. Here you will find shops and a food centre, you can get your hands hennaed, your fortune told by a parrot or dress up in Indian clothes for a photo opportunity.

ⓐ Serangoon Rd ⓝ MRT: Little India; Bus: 64, 65, 114

Serangoon Road

Once past the tidied up areas at the top of the road, Serangoon quickly resolves into a vibrant, living Indian community. Come

🔺 *A typical stall in Little India*

Little India & Arab Street

here on Sunday nights when the migrant workers congregate and you could be in the backstreets of Delhi. Indian department stores, spice grinders, garland makers, cheap Indian music CD sellers, gold jewellery and sari shops, the aromatic perfumes emanating from the many cafés, men selling betelnuts, sex workers peeping out from some of the side streets all make this one of the most unregulated and genuine parts of the island. The people who live, work and worship along this street are remarkably tolerant of the tourists, and there are some amazing restaurants and coffee shops to sample. The most surprising are the fast food places serving tasty authentic food at laughably low prices. ⓐ Serangoon Rd; self guided tours are available from ⓐ 65 Kerbau Rd ⓣ 6329 1772 ⓦ www.spell7.net ⓛ 10.00–16.30 Tues–Sat. There is a charge for hire of headsets ⓝ MRT: Little India; Bus: 64, 65, 114

CULTURE

Istana Kampong Glam

Once the palace of the island's Malay rulers, Kampong Glam has been reclaimed from the crumbling decay of the late 20th century to be a showcase of Malay history and culture on the island. The old colonial house is now a restaurant and in the grounds are exhibits on the Malay film-making industry and a model of a Malay village. Daily cultural shows include Malay dancing, martial arts and music. Pottery making and batik making workshops also take place when there are large enough crowds. ⓐ 85 Sultan Gate ⓣ 6391 0466 ⓦ www.malayheritage.org.sg ⓛ 13.00–18.00 Mon, 10.00–18.00

Tues–Sun; cultural shows: 15.30 Wed, 11.30 Sun Ⓝ MRT: Bugis;
Bus: 7, 32, 51, 63, 80, 145, 197. Admission charge to exhibitions;
entrance to compound is free

Sakaya Muni Buddha Gaya Temple
Better known as the Temple of a Thousand Lights, this strongly
Thai influenced Buddhist temple is dominated by a 300-ton,
15-m (49-ft) tall statue of the Lord Buddha. The base of the
temple is decorated with scenes from the Buddha's life. Inside
the hollow statue is another representation of the Buddha, this
one showing the master reclining. Hundreds of electric lights
decorate the room, giving the temple its common name. You
can get your fortune told here.
ⓐ Race Course Rd Ⓛ 07.00–18.00 Ⓝ MRT: Farrer Park. Small
donation for fortune telling

Sri Srinivasa Perumal Temple
This temple comes into its own at Thaipusam (see pages 14–15)
when the devotees and their families gather to prepare
themselves for the big march to Tank Road. Perumal, the
incarnation of Vishnu to whom the temple is dedicated, is the
god of mercy and preserver of the universe. A temple to Perumal
was first built here in 1885 but the modern building dates back
to the 1960s. The five-tiered *gopuram* (entry gate) covered in
images of Vishnu in his various incarnations was constructed
in 1975.
ⓐ 397 Serangoon Rd Ⓛ 06.00–12.00, 17.00–21.00 Ⓝ MRT:
Farrer Park.

Sri Veeramakaliamman Temple

Dedicated to the Hindu goddess Kali – a complex mixture of annihilation and benevolence and the wife of the god Shiva – this is one of the most popular temples in Singapore. It was originally built in the late 19th century by South Indian labourers who had settled around Buffalo Road, then added to over the years. The enormous Disney-like *gopuram* was constructed in 1987. Visitors to the temple are welcome but should be considerately dressed and remove their shoes. Inside, the various incarnations of the goddess are represented; one shows a necklace of the skulls of her victims, while others show her in more peaceful modes. Also represented here are Kali's sons Murugan and Ganesh, the elephant-headed god. There is always a buzz of activity in the temple, with worshippers

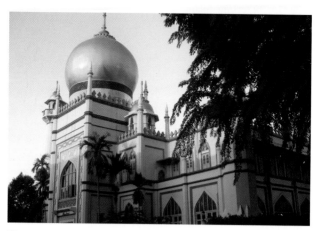
⬢ *Singapore's biggest mosque: Sultan Mosque*

bringing coconuts and bananas to offer the goddess and dhoti-wearing priests attending to them. Often there are wonderful performances of clashing instruments and other events.

ⓐ 141 Serangoon Rd ⓝ MRT: Little India

Sultan Mosque

Singapore's biggest and most central mosque was built in 1925 to a design by English architects Swan and Maclaren. Take away the dome and minarets and there's a distinctly British municipal feel to the place. Visitors can only go into the entrance lobby and must remove shoes and keep shoulders and legs covered. Avoid Fridays when the mosque is very busy.

ⓐ Bussorah St ⓛ 09.00–13.00 ⓝ MRT: Bugis; Bus: 7, 32, 51, 63, 80, 145, 197

DEEPAVALI

The Indian festival of lights sees the area around Serangoon Road come even more alive. The month-long festival, which celebrates an ancient victory of the Hindu god Lord Krishna over a demon called Narakasura, fills the road with decorations and lights. Bazaars selling Indian delicacies and goods spring up in the side streets, and homes are lit with tiny oil lamps as an offering to Lakshmi who will bring prosperity to any house she visits. On the day of the festival Hindus carefully prepare themselves with oil, put on fresh clothes and attend the temple. The festival occurs some time between October and November.

THE CITY

RETAIL THERAPY

Bugis Junction Upmarket shopping centre, incorporating some old streets that are now glass-covered and entirely air-conditioned, with a Japanese department store and more retail outlets than you will have time to visit. Check out the beauty treatments at Missha (02-22) and The Face Shop next door.
🅐 200 Victoria St ☎ 6557 6557 🕐 10.30–21.30 Ⓝ MRT: Bugis

Deemark International labels of men's shirts, formal and casual, at factory prices. A quick look around the other shops in this mall may be worthwhile because prices here are very competitive. 🅐 01-11 Tekka Mall, 2 Serangoon Rd ☎ 6337 4592 🕐 10.00–20.00 Ⓝ MRT: Little India

Jamal Kazura Aromatics Specialist shop selling oils for perfumes and aromatherapy. You can buy the oils in different amounts, from 10 ml to 250 ml, with storage bottles also for sale.
🅐 137 Dunlop St ☎ 6392 1978 🕐 10.00–20.30 Tues–Sun, 12.00–20.30 Mon Ⓝ MRT: Little India

Jyothi Fabrics Silk and lace, mostly from Korea, sold by the metre and varying in price from S$10 to S$300 per metre. There is another outlet, **Manisha: The Fabric Palace**, also in Arab Street (*no. 67*). 🅐 63 Arab St ☎ 6296 4784 🕐 11.00–18.30 Ⓝ MRT: Bugis

MKM Bangles, chokers, gold nosestuds, anklets and costume jewellery – all in a glorious array of colours. 🅐 90 Serangoon Rd ☎ 6294 2903 🕐 10.00–20.30 Ⓝ MRT: Little India

Mustafa Centre An excellent department store, unbeatable for luggage (second floor), which also has a supermarket and pharmacy. This shop is almost a sight in itself, filled with people loading up with suitcases and electrical goods at two in the morning. 📍 145 Syed Alwi Rd 📞 6295 5855 🌐 www.mustafa.com.sg 🕐 24 hours Ⓜ MRT: Farrer Park (Exit A)

Saadullah Carpets from Iran, India and Pakistan. Some are small enough to carry home with you but overseas delivery is also an option. 📍 45 Arab St 📞 6296 8545 🌐 www.tawakacarpets.com 🕐 10.00–20.00 Ⓜ MRT: Bugis

San Marco Collection An attractive shop retailing its own designs in home-made jewellery and precious stones and, as well, a nice line in ethnic clothing from India and Nepal. Come here for that belly dancing outfit you have been looking for. 📍 29 Arab St 📞 6293 3379 🕐 10.00–19.30 Mon–Sat, 12.00–18.00 Sun Ⓜ MRT: Bugis

Sultan Ahmet Lamps, water pipes, cushion and bed covers, ceramics – the merchandise all comes from Turkey. 📍 31 Arab St 📞 6294 6070 🕐 10.00–21.00 Ⓜ MRT: Bugis

Tabletop Creations Facing Sultan Mosque, this store has a good selection of items such as batik fans, bags, scarves and shawls, sets of fancy chopsticks, hand woven baskets and the usual range of T-shirts. Good for small gifts and souvenirs. 📍 46 Bussorah St 📞 6341 7381 🕐 09.00–18.00 Mon–Sat, 09.00–17.00 Sun Ⓜ MRT: Bugis

TAKING A BREAK

Ananda Bhavan £ ❶ First-class vegetarian Indian eatery and, if you order the *paper masala thosai*, you won't get a longer (length, not time) meal anywhere in Singapore. The daily specials are always interesting. Walking from the MRT station towards Serangoon Road, you pass Ananda Bhavan on your right. There is also a branch at 58 Serangoon Road, opposite the Mustafa Centre. ⓐ Blk 663, 01-10 Buffalo Rd ❶ 6294 0684 ⓑ 08.00–20.30 ⓝ MRT: Little India

Blue Oasis £ ❷ A jazzy joint whipping up smoothies and shakes with food like chicken wings, fish and chips, and

⬤ *The popular Blue Oasis in Bussorah Street*

scrambled eggs on toast. Popular with travellers in the neighbourhood's hostels and a pleasant watering hole for a cold beer or glass of wine. ⓐ 60 Bussorah St ⓣ 6396 5905 ⓛ 09.00–21.00 Mon & Sun, Wed–Fri, 11.00–23.00 Sat, closed Tues ⓝ MRT: Bugis

Chola's £ ❸   This is convenient for a quick bite in between shopping at the Mustafa Centre, which is just at the top of the road. Mostly meat dishes but also two vegetarian set meals. Chicken and *biriyanis*, and lots of *dosai*, *utthappam*, *sooji* and *idlies*. ⓐ 115 Syed Alwi Rd St ⓣ 6396 8859 ⓛ 06.00–24.00 ⓝ MRT: Little India

Kampong Glam Café £ ❹   A pleasant place for an iced drink or a traditional Malay dish like *tahu goreng*, *roti kirai* or *gado-gado*. Tables outside on the pavement. ⓐ 17 Bussorah St ⓣ 6294 8923 ⓛ 08.00–24.00 ⓝ MRT: Bugis

Mubarak Restaurant £ ❺   Recommended for a *roti prata* breakfast or mid-morning break, before or after a spot of shopping on Serangoon Road. Tables on the pavement, on the corner of Campbell Lane and Clive Street. ⓐ 21 Campbell Lane ⓣ 6337 1464 ⓛ 06.00–24.00 ⓝ MRT: Little India

AFTER DARK

Restaurants
Blue Jaz £ ❻   Local and Western food plus various smoothies and beers help make this small joint a suitable venue for

relaxing at a pavement table after the sun, and the traffic, has gone down. ⓐ 11 Bali Lane ⓣ 6297 1280 ⓛ 1030–22.30 ⓝ MRT: Bugis

Woodlands £ ⓐ No self-respecting tourist should leave Singapore without visiting the city state's most famous vegetarian restaurant. It offers amazing range of breads served in little steel trays with pots of tongue-lashing curries and a cooling *laksi*. Great. ⓐ 12–14 Upper Dickson Rd ⓣ 6293 6980 ⓛ 07.00–22.30 ⓝ MRT: Little India

Zam Zam Restaurant £ ⓑ This wonderful old Muslim restaurant on North Bridge Road celebrates its centenary in 2008 and, one is inclined to think, the *murtabaks* taste as good as ever. Good value meals and tables upstairs with plenty of room. ⓐ 697 North Bridge Rd ⓣ 6298 7011 ⓛ 08.00–23.00 ⓝ MRT: Bugis

Alaturka ££ ⓒ Turkish and Mediterranean food in a neat little restaurant that makes an effort to evoke a non-Asian atmosphere. Mezzes, kebabs, pide, pizzas and seafood. ⓐ 16 Bussorah St ⓣ 6294 0304 ⓦ www.alaturka.com.sg ⓛ 11.00–23.00 ⓝ MRT: Bugis

Apolo Banana Leaf ££ ⓓ Terrific Indian restaurant with a menu that has stood the test of time. The all-time favourite here is the fish head curry. This is the original branch, in existence since 1974, though there is now also a branch at 48 Serangoon Road. ⓐ 54 Race Course Rd ⓣ 6293 8682 ⓦ www.bananaleafapolo.com ⓛ 10.30–22.30 ⓝ Farrer Park

Olive Tree Restaurant ££ ⓫ Excellent buffet dinner with a gastronomic spread of meat and seafood, although the offerings on Friday and Saturday nights go over the top on seafood. A hearty Champagne brunch on Sunday. ⓐ Hotel Inter-Continental, 80 Middle Rd ⓣ 6825 1061 ⓛ 12.00–14.30 Mon–Fri, 18.00–22.30 Sun–Thur, 11.30–15.30 Sun ⓝ MRT: Bugis

Bars
Prince of Wales Hostel bar with live music Mon–Sat kicking off at 21.30 and a live mic session on Sun nights. Affordable beer. ⓐ 101 Dunlop St ⓣ 6299 0130 ⓦ www.pow.com.sg ⓝ MRT: Bugis or Little India

CHIJMES ££ ⓬
Chijmes is a one-stop, evening food-and-drink venue where there is a good choice of restaurants and themed pubs, plus an open area with a large screen showing international sports fixtures. The best restaurant for Mediterranean-style food is the candlelit **Esmirada**; you should not be disappointed by the skewered meat, seafood paella or the mussels.
ⓐ 30 Victoria St ⓣ 6336 3684 ⓦ www.esmirada.com
ⓛ 18.00–22.30 Sun–Thur, 18.00–23.00 Fri & Sat
ⓝ MRT: City Hall

THE CITY

Boat Quay & Chinatown

Once the commercial hub of the city, this area has long since
abandoned its bumboats and *coolie wallahs* for designer
restaurants and cool bars. Its huge, once-crumbling warehouses
now provide a playground for the young and restless, and the
elderly public buildings of the British Empire have been given a
shiny makeover and turned over to the tourist trade. Like Arab
Street and Serangoon Road, the whole lifestyle of the area has
been packaged into easy-to-chew bites of colourful Chinese life.
But sneak past the tourist itinerary and you'll find a little of the
old ways – strange things in tubs waiting to become dinner,
paper products to burn for the ancestors, weird and wonderful
medicinal items, fire walking in the temples, and shops where
some serious bargaining, Chinese style, is *de rigueur*.

SIGHTS & ATTRACTIONS

Amoy Street
Once densely populated by people from the Xiamen province
of China, the street has mostly undergone some serious
gentrification. Where once tiny shops spilled their wares out
onto the five foot ways (see page 49), now trendy businesses
have renovated the old shophouses. Some of them have been
beautifully done, and you can see the bat-shaped ventilation
grills, red doors and symbols warding off the bad *chi* that travels
in straight lines along the streets. On the corner of Amoy Street
(*no. 66*) is a still active place of worship, the Sin Chor Kung
temple, painted bright red to draw in some good luck, and

guarded by two stone lions and some huge pots of ash from
burned incense sticks.

Far East Square

Entirely constructed as part of the renovation of Chinatown, this
area, with the Fuk Tak Chi temple at its heart, has become a
major lunch stop for busy office workers. The food halls bear
little resemblance, either in atmosphere or cost, to the hawker
centres of old but they are air-conditioned and very popular.

Sago Street

This street was once the very heart of Chinatown. It was home
for decades to death houses, places where the very elderly were
taken to die, and contained both the death houses themselves
and several coffin makers. It was part of Chinese belief that

◗ *The Boat Quay area is very colourful*

Boat Quay & Chinatown

0   300 metres

0   300 yards

having someone die in the home was bad luck so the elderly, one assumes, cheerfully went off to these places. Now gentrified, the street comes alive during Chinese New Year when it is filled with stalls and decorations. Perhaps as a memory to the thousands of elderly people who came here to die, a little concrete seating area, Trishaw Park, provides a quiet spot to meet and chat. Seriously dedicated visitors can hire a rickshaw here for a trip around the area. As it morphs into Trengganu Street, you will see that some of the old businesses struggle on. Trengganu Street was once a red light area, home to Japanese prostitutes. At the corner with Smith Street is Lai Chun Yuen, a former Cantonese opera house which still retains much of its original architecture. On the opposite corner is the Chinatown Complex market and food centre, where you can stroll around the wetmarket and be amazed at what the locals

▲ *Junction of Smith and Trengganu streets*

are buying for dinner. Here you may well catch sight of a bill being tallied with an abacus. In some of the backstreets around here (Smith Street, Kreta Ayer Road, Keong Saik Road) you will see what at first seems completely mad – household goods made entirely of bamboo sticks covered in tissue paper and painted. These are still very popular gifts for the departed. The paper goods are burned and their essence floats up in the smoke to provide for the ancestors. Here you will see Mercedes cars, laptops, Philippina maids, washing machines, men's suits, three-piece suites, credit cards – if it exists on Earth and brings its owner status, then you can buy it here.

South Bridge Road

This very busy main street is the economic heart of Chinatown. Like the rest of Chinatown its traditional small shops are giving way to renovated tourist-orientated boutiques selling antiques and designer nicknacks for the modern home. A few of the older residents hang in there, and the street is home to the Sri Mariamman Hindu Temple and the Eu Yan Sang Medical Hall, both places that have resisted the tidying up of the area.

CULTURE

Chinatown Heritage Centre

If you only visit one of Singapore's museums you should make it this one. The 200 or so years of Chinese immigration into Singapore has been collected into this fascinating museum, made up of three renovated shophouses. A journey through the museum, accompanied by a soundtrack of period music and the noise of the shophouses, starts off with a model of one of the junks that the immigrant workers arrived in and goes on to tell of their safe landing and settlement in this area. Using personal accounts by Chinese residents whose memories go back to the early years of the last century, the museum recreates much of what has been lost in the gentrification of the area – the history of the clan associations, the wars between rival secret societies, the work in the quays and other places. Whole rooms are recreated, including one of the Sago Street death houses, and the terrible living conditions of the workers are brought home. On a lighter note there are original hawker stalls, a coffee shop and lots of things familiar to older visitors – toys made in Singapore, adverts for commodities from the 1950s and much more.

🅐 48 Pagoda St 🅣 6325 2878 🆆 www.chinatownheritage.com.sg 🅛 09.00–20.00 Mon–Thur, 09.00–21.00 Fri–Sun 🅝 MRT: Chinatown. Admission charge (free guided tours)

Eu Yan Sang Medical Hall

Dispensers of traditional Chinese medicine, medical halls were once the main form of medical treatment available to the poor of Singapore. Eu Yan Sang started off his business in Perak in 1879, and expanded first to Singapore in 1910 then as far as Hong Kong and China. Part tourist attraction and part medicine shop, the three renovated art deco shophouses are filled with all sorts of dried and preserved things you really wouldn't want to eat but which, apparently, are very good for you – lizards, scorpions, snakes, all manner of dried fungus, internal (and external!) organs of assorted creatures and, of course, ginseng, which is doled out to visitors in the form of tea. Whatever your complaint there is a cure and since the place has been operating for more than 100 years you can probably trust that the cure won't do you any harm. Probably.

ⓐ 267–71 South Bridge Rd ☎ 6223 6333 ⏱ 08.30–18.00 Mon–Sat, closed Sun Ⓜ MRT: Chinatown

Fu Tak Chi Museum
Beautifully renovated, this former temple was established by the Hakka community in the early 19th century and functioned well into the late 20th century. It is a lovely building, its decorated roof and interior door gods well preserved, but is now a museum to the old ways of Chinatown. Displays include a diorama of what this area once looked like, opium-smoking paraphernalia, old clothes and a model of a junk. It's not up to the standard of the Chinatown Heritage Centre, but as a well lit example of a temple building it's well worth a visit.

ⓐ Telok Ayer Street ⏱ 10.00–22.00 Mon–Thur, 09.00–21.00 Fri–Sun Ⓜ MRT: Raffles Place

Sri Mariamman Temple
This is Singapore's oldest Hindu temple, built before the island was divided into ethnic quarters and founded by Naraina Pillay, an Indian official who arrived in Singapore aboard the same vessel as Raffles. The brick building was erected in 1843 and is dedicated to Mariamman, the goddess of healing. Other gods figure here, as they do in other Hindu temples. At the left of the entrance is Krishna and at the right is Rama, while the gold figure at the bottom of the frieze is Mariamman. Inside, the

walls and ceiling are covered in pictures of assorted deities and there are shrines to Periachiamman, to whom small babies are brought for protection, and Sri Aravan. During the Thimithi Festival devotees to the goddess in their hundreds line up to run barefoot across hot coals inside the temple. If you are here during the festival be prepared for big crowds and a lot of yelling. ⓐ South Bridge Road ⓒ 06.00–12.30, 16.00–21.30 ⓝ MRT: Chinatown; Bus: 2, 12, 33, 51, 61, 62, 63, 81, 84, 103, 124, 143, 145, 147, 166, 174, 190, 197, 851. Charge for camera usage.

Thian Hock Keng Temple
This temple in Telok Ayer Street is the oldest Taoist temple in Singapore and is dedicated to Tin Hou, the goddess who protects seafarers. Its name translates into the Temple of Heavenly Happiness. When it was built it occupied a prime site on the waterfront and would have been the first place that Hokkien travellers came to thank the deities for their safe arrival. The current building was begun in 1839 when the statue of the goddess was brought in from southern China. The elaborate roof tiles are delft and the supporting pillars, like the goddess, come from southern China. The railings are from Glasgow. Stone lions guard the doors and all manner of wildlife is incorporated into the roof. The courtyard of the temple is where lots of the paper goods begin their ascent to the afterlife. Next door to the temple is a tiny patch of green called Telok Sayer Green and next door again is the Nagore Durgha shrine, built by southern Indian Chulias.
ⓐ Telok Ayer Street ⓒ 08.30–21.00 ⓝ MRT: Chinatown; Bus: 2, 12, 33, 51, 61, 62, 63, 81, 84, 103, 124, 143, 145, 147, 166, 174, 190, 197, 851

URA Gallery

This government-owned exhibition space might seem a little dull at first glance but is actually quite fascinating. It contains an exhibition of Singapore's plans for urban renewal, and considering the determination, cash and engineering that gets put into Singapore's schemes it is well worth a visit to be amazed. The exhibition demonstrates just how much of what you take for granted as Singapore was once the open sea. New land reclamation projects, urban renewal schemes and plans for renovating places of historical significance are all laid out in a series of interactive displays. You can also plan your own little bit of the city and play around with the webcam above the building. You'll find yourself torn between admiration for the scope of it all and despair at just how controlled and regulated this tiny city state is.

🄰 45 Maxwell Rd 🄣 6321 8321 🄦 www.ura.gov.sg 🄲 09.00–16.00 Mon–Fri, 09.00–12.30 Sat, closed Sun 🄽 MRT: Chinatown

RETAIL THERAPY

Nail Embassy Manicures start at S$25 and there are various other treatments, including waxing. Appointments are not always essential, except on Sundays. Easy to find, near the corner of Erskine Road and South Bridge Road. 🄰 33 Erskine Rd 🄣 6227 1070 🄲 11.00–21.00 Mon–Fri, 11.00–20.00 Sat, 11.00–19.00 Sun 🄽 MRT: Outram Park

Pagoda Street Good for souvenirs, gifts, T-shirts and the like. Some schlock but also places like Scarlet Thread (*no. 57*), a

superior art and craft shop. ⓐ Pagoda St ⏱ 10.00–23.00
ⓝ MRT: Chinatown

Sago Street Best to stroll down here at night when the street is
pedestrianised and the stalls are out on the pavement. Come
here for Chinese slippers, jade wristbands, jewellery and silk
garments that will make you look like a Singapore Airlines
hostess. Nothing here is expensive, and prices are mostly
marked and more-or-less fixed. ⓐ Sago St ⏱ 10.00–23.00
ⓝ MRT: Chinatown

TAKING A BREAK

Maxwell Food Centre £ ❶ One of the few unreconstructed
food centres in central Singapore, complete with whirling fans.
Some very slithery tastes from the Chinese outlets – a
noticeboard outside explains some of the more exotic
concoctions. Vegetarian food can be found at Mr Bean (*no. 11*),
and at no. 37. There is also an Indian outlet serving *murtabaks*
and *roti*. ⓐ Maxwell Rd ⏱ 08.30–20.30 ⓝ MRT: Chinatown or
Outram Park

Ya Kun £ ❷ The original Ya Kun coffee shop in what is now a
chain of similarly named premises. The menu here is identical,
except for the prices, to the one that first greeted customers in
1944. Be sure to try the Ya Kun toast with an egg to dip it in.
Tables indoors and out. ⓐ 01-01 Far East Square, 18 China St
☎ 6438 3638 ⓦ www.yakun.com ⏱ 07.30–19.00 Mon–Fri,
08.00–17.00 Sat & Sun ⓝ MRT: Chinatown

AFTER DARK

Restaurants

Singapore Heritage Restaurant £ ❸ A bit kitschy but a likeable and inoffensive café that serves up old Chinese favourites like chilli crab sauce but adds spaghetti just for fun. The satay and mango chicken rice are well worth tasting. ⓐ 46 Pagoda St ❶ 6225 2001 ⓛ 11.00–23.00 Ⓝ MRT: Chinatown

Jerry's ££ ❹ Jerry's is the place for ribs and steaks. Space is limited, so make a reservation, either indoors or outside on the five foot ways pavement under two slowly whirling fans. Cocktails and world beers available. ⓐ 92 Club St ❶ 6323 4550 ⓦ www.jerrybbq.com.sg ⓛ 12.00–22.00 Ⓝ MRT: Chinatown

Majestic Restaurant ££ ❺ Serves cutting-edge Cantonese food, such as crispy wasabi prawns and Peking duck served with spiced foie gras. The décor is equally modern, with an open kitchen design and dining tables under ceiling portholes that look up into the hotel's swimming pool. ⓐ New Majestic Hotel, 31 Bukit Pasoh Rd ❶ 6511 4700 ⓛ 12.00–14.30, 18.30–22.00 Ⓝ MRT: Chinatown

Senso ££ ❻ Italian fine dining in an alfresco courtyard setting or indoors in air-conditioned comfort. Either way you will enjoy well-prepared Italian dishes like fettuccine with lobster in a fragrant herb sauce. A modernist bar serves cocktails and aperitifs. Ⓝ 21 Club St ❶ 6224 3534 ⓛ 12.00–14.30 & 18.00–22.30 Mon–Fri, 18.00–22.30 Sat & Sun Ⓝ MRT: Chinatown

Ember Restaurant ££–£££ ❼ Advance booking is fairly essential at this popular European restaurant where the food, décor and style of service is all very contemporary. ⓐ Hotel 1929, 50 Keong Saik Rd ❶ 6347 1928 ● 11.30–14.00, 18.30–22.00 Ⓜ MRT: Chinatown

Bars & clubs

Ministry of Sound The London megaclub has reached Singapore. There is a similar mix of music in the various rooms – electro, house, trance and hip hop – and big-name DJs enliven this sonic supermarket. ⓐ 01-02 Block C, The Cannery, Clarke Quay ❶ 6235 2292 Ⓦ www.ministryofsound.com.sg ● 21.00–04.00 Wed–Sat, closed Sun–Tues Ⓜ MRT: Clarke Quay

Roof Bar Unsophisticated but friendly, the Roof Bar serves beer by the mug or jug as well as wine and spirits. Great views of the festivities during Chinese New Year. ⓐ 32A Pagoda St ❶ 9392 0360 Ⓦ www.roofbarsundeckterrace.com ● 17.00–24.00 Mon–Sat, closed Sun Ⓜ MRT: Chinatown

Zouk Well-established nightclub that now comprises three venues – Phuture, Velvet Underground and Zouk itself – and continues to attract a hip crowd. There is a happy hour on Friday & Saturday between 23.00 and 24.00. ⓐ 17 Jiak Kim St ❶ 6738 2988 Ⓦ www.zoukclub.com.sg ● 21.00–04.00 Wed, Fri & Sat, closed Sun–Thur Ⓜ MRT: Clarke Quay; Bus: 54 (from Scotts Rd), 32, 195 (from City Hall MRT station)

❶ *A quiet beach on the island of Sentosa*

Sentosa & Western Singapore

To the west of the island, beyond the waves of high-rise public housing and modern town centres, there are several places to visit. The Singapore Science Centre will keep children busy for hours, while the Jurong Bird Park is a genuinely fascinating place. Haw Par Villa, renovated, failed and renovated again, is a shadow of its former self but worth the trip for the grisly scenes of damnation portrayed in its concrete statues. Sentosa defies description and just has to be visited. A law should be passed that no one can leave Singapore until they've spent a day there. Closer to home Holland Village is a shopper's dream, while the Botanic Gardens, near Orchard Road, makes a pleasant day out.

◔ *Cacti in the Cactus Garden at the Botanic Gardens*

SIGHTS & ATTRACTIONS

Botanic Gardens

Carefully manicured, sporting all manner of weird and wonderful plants (make sure you spot the cannon ball trees!), the Botanic Gardens is a great place to visit. Come early in the morning to watch the tai chi exercises; come at dusk to venture into the tiny patch of virgin rainforest and imagine you're in the jungle; or just turn up in the middle of the day and wander. Best of all is the orchid garden filled with the most exotic orchids, many of them bred here and sporting names dumped on them to honour visiting foreign dignitaries. Afterwards pop out to the hawker centre at the main gate where to savour what is possibly the best *roti john* and *tahu goreng* in town.

ⓐ Holland Rd ⓛ 05.00–24.00; National Orchid Garden 08.30–19.00 ⓝ Bus: 7, 75, 77, 105, 106, 123, 174. Admission charge for orchid garden

HarbourFront & Mount Faber

The best way to visit Sentosa, be scared witless and see some brilliant views at the same time is to arrive by cable-car from Mount Faber. This has the added advantage of a visit to Mount

Opening in early 2007, but not due to be completed until 2010, is the new, expensive monorail system which will be the fastest way for visitors to arrive at the various locations on Sentosa. HarbourFront Station will be the first to open; the three other stops may take a little longer.

Singapore region

0 ___ 4 km
0 ___ 2 miles

Johor Bahru

Sembawang

MALAYSIA

Sungei Buloh Nature Park

Woodlands

Kranji Reservoir

Mandai

Sarimbun Reservoir

Murai Reservoir

Kranji War Cemetery

Singapore Zoo & Night Safari

Lim Chu Kang 57

Seletar Reservoir

Choa Chu Kang

Lim Chu Kang

Bukit Panjang

Lower Peirce Reservoir

Selat Johor

Poyan Reservoir

Choa Chu Kang 88

Memories at Old Ford Factory

Bukit Timah 162

Upper Peirce Reservoir

Bukit Timah Nature Reserve

Tengeh Reservoir

Peng Kang 61

Bukit Batok

Snow City

Bukit Timah

MacRitchie Reservoir

Tiger Brewery

Tuas

Jurong

Singapore Science Centre

Holland Village

Jurong Bird Park

Pandan Reservoir

Clementi

Botanic Gardens

Selat Jurong

National University of Singapore

Queenstown

Pasir Panjing

Haw Par Villa

Jurong Island

Mount Faber & Cable Car Station

Selat Pandan

HarbourFront

Fort Siloso

Sentosa Island

N

106

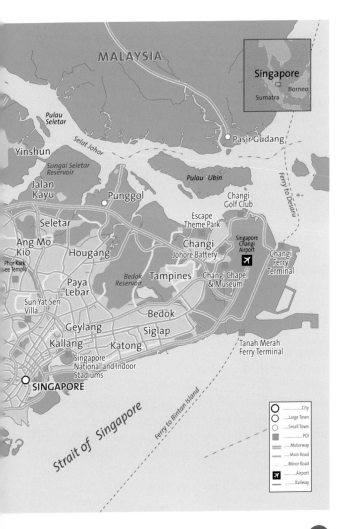

MALAYSIA

Singapore

Borneo

Sumatra

Pulau
Seletar

Selat Johor

Pasir Gudang

Yinshun

Sungai Seletar
Reservoir

Pulau Ubin

Ferry to Desaru

Jalan
Kayu

Punggol

Changi
Golf Club

Seletar

Escape
Theme Park

Singapore
Changi
Airport

Ang Mo
Kio

Hougang

Changi

Changi
Ferry
Terminal

Phor Kark
see Temple

Johore Battery

Paya
Lebar

Bedok
Reservoir

Tampines

Changi Chapel
& Museum

Sun Yat Sen
Villa

Bedok

Geylang

Siglap

Kallang

Katong

Tanah Merah
Ferry Terminal

Singapore
National and Indoor
Stadiums

SINGAPORE

Strait of Singapore

Ferry to Bintan Island

	City
	Large Town
	Small Town
	POI
	Motorway
	Main Road
	Minor Road
	Airport
	Railway

107

Faber, which is worth the effort for the pretty park at the top of the hill. The easiest route to Mount Faber is via the cable-car from the HarbourFront, a huge new development of shops, marine terminals and restaurants – claimed to be the largest single shopping centre in Singapore, although how long that will last is anybody's guess.

Ⓝ Bus: 30, 65, 80, 97, 100, 145, 166, 855 to Telok Blangah Rd; cable-car to Mount Faber from HarbourFront Tower 2: 08.30–23.00

Holland Village

Once the shopping centre for British troops stationed in army housing estates all around, Holland Village still retains a much more *gweilo*-orientated tone than some of the other suburbs of the city. The place is awash with craft, furniture and antique shops, as well as some good discount electrical stores. An afternoon shopping here, taking in lunch at one of the cafés or in the wetmarket, can be followed by an evening's entertainment in one of the several bars.

Jurong Bird Park

Hundreds of species of birds, many of them roaming free, live in this huge park. A whole day can be spent here, visiting the various houses, the walk-through aviary and the bird shows. When you arrive be sure to note down the times of the shows and get to them – they are fascinating and because of the size of the place they are easy to miss. ⓐ 2 Jurong Hill ⓣ 6265 0022 ⓦ www.birdpark.com.sg ⓛ 09.00–18.00 Ⓝ MRT: Boon Lay; Bus: 194, 251. Admission charge

Sentosa

It may not be an earthly paradise, but it couldn't be anywhere
else than Singapore. This place is how Singaporeans like their
fun – organised, noisy, crowded and in the worst possible taste.
If your idea of a good time is a night at the theatre followed by
supper and a quiet glass of wine, don't come here. If you like
history, fun fairs, water rides, tacky souvenir shops and dancing
fountains, this place is essential. Underwater World is a truly
fascinating experience. Strangely there are also areas of
undisturbed wildlife, empty beaches and some very classy
hotels. Ⓝ Sentosa bus from HarbourFront 07.00–23.00
Sun–Thur, 07.00–00.30 Fri & Sat; SIA hop-on hop-off bus from
Clarke Quay 10.00–18.00; cable-car from Mount Faber and
HarbourFront Tower 2: 08.30–23.00. Admission charge to island
and to each sight

◑ Loris feeding at Jurong Bird Park

CULTURE

Fort Siloso

Here you'll find a series of coastal fortifications built by the British and occupied by them from the 1880s until they were surrendered to the Japanese in 1942, when Sentosa became a prisoner of war camp and base for the Japanese. The story of the fort is presented in an entertaining way; what's more, there are tunnels to wander, big guns and some great views.

ⓐ 33 Allanbrooke Rd, Sentosa ⓣ 6276 0388
ⓦ www.sentosa.com.sg ⓛ 10.00–18.00 ⓝ Bus to Sentosa/cable-car, then Blue Green, Red bus line, then Fort Train. Admission charge

Haw Par Villa

Built by the brothers who marketed Tiger Balm oil, this is a theme park with a difference. Hundreds of concrete statues portray the horrors that will befall sinners in the many layers of hell. Just to cheer you up are more statues of good things happening in heaven plus some weird and wonderful creatures, but it's the torture images that will stay with you. Kids love it.

ⓐ 262 Pasir Panjang Rd ⓣ 6872 2780 ⓛ 09.00–19.00
ⓝ MRT: Buona Vista, then bus 200

Images of Singapore Exhibition

An interactive history of Singapore with wax figures in traditional costumes, leading figures in the island's history dioramas, all culminating in the Surrender Chambers where the history of World War II and the final surrender of the Japanese is

recounted. This is Singapore as it wants to be seen. Fascinating.
ⓐ Sentosa ⓣ 1800 736 8672 ⓦ www.sentosa.com.sg
ⓛ 09.00–19.00 ⓝ Sentosa bus from HarbourFront; SIA hop-on
bus from Clarke Quay; cable-car from Mount Faber and
HarbourFront Tower 2. Admission charge

Singapore Science Centre
Like all good science centres, this one has knobs to pull, screens
to press, huge pieces of noisy moving equipment and hours of
fascinating engagement with the physical world. It also has
plagues of schoolchildren, just like all the other science centres
you've ever been to. Good fun, but avoid school hours. The
Omnimax Theatre shows scary movies on an enormous screen.
ⓐ 15 Science Centre Rd ⓣ 6425 2500 ⓦ www.science.edu.sg
ⓛ 10.00–18.00 Tues–Thur, Sat & Sun, 10.00–21.00 Fri, closed
Mon. Omnimax 10.00–20.00 Tues–Sun, closed Mon ⓝ MRT:
Jurong East; Bus: 66, 178, 198, 335. Admission charge for Science
Centre and Omnimax

Tiger Brewery
The brewery making the famous beer of Singapore, which
perfumes the air of Jurong and cools the palate in so many
hawker centres, is open to the public (in groups of ten or turn
up/phone and hope to join one already organised). Be prepared
for a movie about the company and its history, a tour through the
shiny high-tech works and several hours in the bar checking that
the brew is just right. ⓐ 459 Jalan Ahmad Ibrahim ⓣ 6860 3007
ⓦ www.apb.com.sg/breweryTour.html ⓛ Tours: 10.30, 14.00, 16.00
ⓝ MRT: Boon Lay, then bus 182. Admission charge

RETAIL THERAPY

Lim's Art & Living Singapore has a reputation for excellent arts and crafts. Lim's has an illustrious history, dating back to the 1960s when it started selling Asian artefacts to British troops, and is still one of the best places for decorative items for the home. ⓐ 02-01 Holland Rd Shopping Centre, 211 Holland Avenue ⓣ 6467 1300 ⓛ 10.00–20.30 Ⓝ MRT: Buona Vista

Vico City Singapore's latest retail destination, convenient to visit when travelling to or from Sentosa; it has more than 300 outlets devoted to shopping, eating and drinking, and entertainment. Marks & Spencer and Tangs are two of the big-name tenants; there is also a multiplex cinema and an outdoor amphitheatre on the third level with fine views of the offshore scene. ⓐ HarbourFront ⓣ 6469 5647 ⓛ 10.00–20.30 Ⓝ MRT: HarbourFront

Vista & Co Following in the footsteps of Lim's Art & Living, this is another shop in the Holland Village neighbourhood with attractive Asian-style items such as Chinese opera masks, mahjong sets, bead curtains and porcelain lamp stands. ⓐ 02-30 Holland Rd Shopping Centre, 211 Holland Avenue ⓣ 6466 6276 ⓣ 10.00–20.30 Ⓝ MRT: Buona Vista

TAKING A BREAK

Crystal Jade Kitchen £ A suitable venue for a speedy Chinese lunch, with a choice of delicious *dim sum*, fried spring rolls,

noodles and *congee*. ❸ 2 Lorong Mambong, Holland Village
❶ 6475 8174 ❷ 09.30–21.00 ❹ MRT: Buona Vista

New Zealand Natural £ For delicious ice creams made of 100 per
cent natural ingredients, plus smoothies, fruit juices, waffles,
visit Sentosa's branch of the trendy international chain of ice
cream parlours. ❸ 50 Siloso Walk Beach, Sentosa ❶ 6273 1971
❿ www.nzn.com.sg ❹ Sentosa bus from HarbourFront; SIA
hop-on bus from Clarke Quay; cable-car from Mount Faber and
HarbourFront Tower 2

San Katong Laksa £ An informal setting for the enjoyment
of *laksa*, a filling noodle soup with dried shrimps, coconut
milk, slices of fishcake and prawns. Good local coffee too.
❸ 29B Lorong Liput, Holland Village ❶ 6475 8045 ❷ 09.30–22.00
❹ MRT: Buona Vista

Thai Express £ Tasty bites like Thai fried squid, *popiah* wraps and
clever concoctions with tofu help give plenty of choice to all
comers. ❸ 16 Lorong Mambong, Holland Village ❶ 6475 8021
❷ 09.30–22.00 ❹ MRT: Buona Vista

AFTER DARK

Restaurants
Baden Restaurant and Pub ££ A long-established German-style
restaurant where, once you step into the dark teakwood interior,
the Orient feels like a continent away. Tuck into steak or pork
knuckles washed down with jugs of Bavarian beer. ❸ 42 Lorong

Mambong, Holland Village ☎ 6475 1270 🕐 18.30–22.30 Ⓜ MRT:
Buona Vista

Michelangelo's ££ Upmarket Italian restaurant patronised by
the local expat community who come here for the vodka penne
before a main course and a tiramisu and brownies afterwards.
🅐 01-60 Block 44 Chip Bee Gardens, Jalan Merah Saga, Holland
Village ☎ 6475 9069 🕐 11.30–14.30 & 18.30–23.00 Sun–Fri,
18.30–23.00 Sat Ⓜ MRT: Buona Vista

Original Sin ££ A vegetarian and vegan restaurant, with
signature dishes of risotto, *bosco misto* (tofu patties) and a
mezze platter. 🅐 01-62 Block 43 Chip Bee Gardens, Jalan Merah
Saga, Holland Village ☎ 6475 5605 🕐 11.30–14.30 & 18.30–23.00
Tues–Sun, closed Mon Ⓜ MRT: Buona Vista

Min Jiang ££–£££ The large-sized bungalows of Rochester Park
were once home to British officers – the lower ranks were
crowded into Chip Bee Gardens – and have now been converted
into classy restaurants. Min Jiang's speciality is Beijing Duck
prepared in a wood-fired oven. 🅐 5 Rochester Park ☎ 6774 0122
🕐 11.00–14.30, 18.00–22.30 Ⓜ MRT: Buona Vista

Sky Dining £££ For a meal with a difference, splash out on a
three-course meal in a cable-car, while it glides 70m above the
sea between Mount Faber and Sentosa. Western and
continental set meals. The journey starts from The Jewel Box on
Mount Faber. Advance reservation essential. Children's menu
available. 🅐 The Jewel Box, 109 Mount Faber Rd ☎ 6377 9688

Ⓦ www.mountfaber.com.sg/main-skydining.htm Ⓛ 18.30–20.30
Ⓝ cable-car from HarbourFront Tower 2; Bus: Parks 409 (Sat, Sun
& public holidays)

Clubs
Wala Wala Café Bar One of the most popular nightspots in
Holland Village, with an outdoor scene on the first level and live
music up above. Ⓐ 31 Lorong Mambong, Holland Village
Ⓣ 7829 8934 Ⓛ 18.30–23.00 Ⓝ MRT: Buona Vista

ACCOMMODATION

Costa Sands Resort ££ If you fancy a night in Sentosa at
reasonable prices try this place – huts and chalets, pool, café,
barbecue pits and all the fun of Sentosa. Ⓐ 30 Imbiah Walk,
Sentosa Ⓣ 6235 1666 Ⓦ www.costasands.com.sg Ⓝ Sentosa bus
from HarbourFront; SIA hop-on bus from Clarke Quay; cable-car
from Mount Faber and HarbourFront Tower 2

Rasa Sentosa Shangri La ££–£££ All the Shangri La luxury plus
spa, beachfront accommodation, water sports, pool, Jacuzzi,
gym, etc. Ⓐ 101 Siloso Rd, Sentosa Ⓣ 6235 1666 Ⓦ www.shangri-
la.com Ⓝ Sentosa bus from HarbourFront; SIA hop-on bus from
Clarke Quay; cable-car from Mount Faber and HarbourFront
Tower

Bukit Timah, Changi & Bintan

In the northern and eastern areas of Singapore, all readily accessible by public transport in around 30 minutes, you'll find places to explore wildlife as well as some notable reminders of the island's role in World War II. The wildlife comes either neatly packaged at the zoo, or in its raw state at the Bukit Timah Nature Reserve or on Pulau Ubin, the perfect antidote to urban blues or consumer blow-out. Bukit Timah tends to be only mildly busy at weekends and public holidays; Singapore's zoo is always full and, despite some enlightened aspects to its keeping and caging of animals, is still a zoo. Or, if you really want to get away from Singapore, why not visit Indonesia? From a ferry terminal at the eastern end of Singapore it is just a one-hour journey to the island of Bintan and, once there, you will really feel you are in Asia.

SIGHTS & ATTRACTIONS

Bintan

All you need is your passport and a US$10 note (for a visa) – obtainable from a money exchange at the ferry terminal – and you can be on Bintan in an hour. The island has a number of resort hotels, all owned and managed by Singaporean companies, where you can sunbathe under swaying palm trees, engage in water sports or indulge yourself at a luxury spa. The resort hotels all have their transport waiting at the arrival ferry terminal, and urban-weary travellers will soon find themselves in what the brochures call a 'sun-kissed paradise for fun-seekers'.

Tanah Merah ferry Terminal ☏ 6542 4369 ⓦ www.brf.com.sg
🕐 Ferries run from 09.05–20.15 Mon–Thur, 08.05–20.00 Fri,
08.05–20.00 Sat & Sun

Bukit Timah Nature Reserve

The 164-m (538-ft) high Bukit Timah Hill, in central Singapore, is
home to an area of primary rainforest within the city's limits –
one of only two such places in the world (the other being Rio de
Janeiro). What's more, it claims to have more plant species than
the whole of North America. It certainly has macaques, snakes,
giant ants, raucous bird life, monitor lizards, scorpions and
pangolins, any of which you could well encounter while
wandering the well-signposted walkways. Go early in the

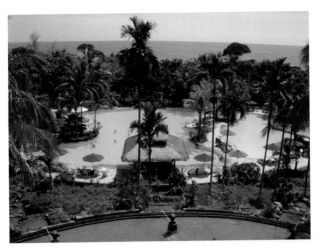

🔺 *Escape to one of Bintan's lagoon resorts*

morning when the wildlife is at its best, before the heat becomes oppressive and the place fills up with joggers.
ⓐ 177 Hindehede Drive ⓣ 1800 468 5736 ⓦ www.nparks.gov.sg
ⓛ Visitor centre: 08.30 –18.00 ⓝ Bus: 67, 75, 170, 171, 173, 184, 852, 961

Changi Chapel & Museum

A harrowing account in the words, photographs and artwork of some of those internees lucky enough to have survived the Japanese occupation of the island. Here also is a replica of the chapel built by inmates, and lots of messages left by those who lost family and friends here. ⓐ 1000 Upper Changi Rd
ⓣ 6214 2451 ⓦ www.changimuseum.com ⓛ 09.30–16.00 ⓝ MRT: Tanah Merah, then bus 2; Bus: 2, 29

Joo Chiat Road

Beautifully restored Peranakan shophouses, especially those at the junction of Koon Seng Road, with shops selling all manner of things you'd like to take home. In the Joo Chiat Complex there are glorious inexpensive silks, batik and carpets.
ⓝ MRT: Eunos; Bus: 15, 16, 33, 155

Kranji War Cemetery

The burial ground of Allied soldiers and the memorial that commemorates the thousands who died is a moving sight. Also here are the tombs of two former presidents of Singapore.
ⓐ 9 Woodlands Rd ⓛ 07.00–18.00 ⓝ MRT: Kranji; Bus: 170

Memories at Old Ford Factory

At the beautifully restored factory where Lt General Percival handed Singapore over to the Japanese in 1942 is an account of life in Singapore under Japanese occupation told through stories collected by the National Archives. The room where the surrender document was signed is the most powerful exhibit. ⓐ 351 Upper Bukit Timah Rd ⓣ 6332 7973 ⓦ www.s1942.org.sg ⓛ 09.00–17.30 Mon–Fri, 09.00–13.30 Sat, closed Sun ⓝ Bus: 67, 75, 171, 173, 178, 184, 961, 170. Admission charge for video

Pulau Ubin

Pulau Ubin has more in common with a rural backwater in Malaysia than anywhere you would associate with Singapore, and a visit to the island is invariably a charming journey of discovery for most visitors. *Kampong* houses nestle in banana groves, with chickens running around and the occasional pig or goat rustling in the undergrowth. There are no cars and so far no plans to develop what must be a prime piece of real estate. The ideal way to get around is by bike, which can be hired from various shops such as Comfort Bicycle Rental (ⓣ 9008 1357), beside the boat jetty. There are places to eat near the jetty but take plenty of water on your cycle or trek around the island. Just as much fun is the bumboat ride out there.
ⓐ Pulau Ubin ⓣ 6542 7944 ⓝ Bus: 2 from Victoria St or Tanah Merah to Changi Village, then a boat from the nearby Changi Ferry Terminal (07.00–19.00 to the island)

Singapore Zoo & Night Safari

As zoos go, this one is exemplary – happy-looking animals in large enclosures, an endangered species breeding programme, and good contact between customer and exhibit. The animal shows are good fun and there are lots of things to engage younger visitors. The Night Safari adds the mystery of the dark to the enclosed animals. Wander around barely lit pathways to see nocturnal animals or take the tram ride through the various terrains set up in the park.

ⓐ 80 Mandai Lake Rd ⓣ 6269 3411 ⓦ www.zoo.com.sg ⓛ Zoo: 08.30–18.00; Night Safari: 19.30–24.00 ⓜ MRT: Ang Mo Kio, then bus 138; Bus: 138, 171, 927. Admission charge for both sights

🔺 Phor Kark See Temple

CULTURE

Phor Kark See Temple

Stretching over 8 hectares (19 acres) and standing out against the skyline with its multicoloured and decorated roofs, this Buddhist temple is quite modern but still fascinating to wander around. The monastery includes a library, refectory, crematorium, turtle ponds, pagodas and huge statues of the Buddha and Kuan Yin, the goddess of mercy. If the place seems a little familiar it is because several kung fu movies have been filmed using it as a backdrop.

ⓐ 88 Bright Hill Drive ⓛ 07.00–18.00 ⓝ MRT: Bishan; Bus: 130

Sun Yat Sen Villa

A sight for lovers of Chinese history, this villa (near Toa Payoh) was home for a time to Dr Sun Yat Sen, who had a role to play in the Chinese revolution. You'll find pictures of Dr Sun rousing the tin miners of Malaysia, displays about his life and the history of the villa.

ⓐ 12 Tai Gi Rd ⓣ 6256 7377 ⓦ www.wanqingyuan.com.sg ⓛ 09.00–17.00 Tues–Sun ⓝ MRT: Toa Payoh; Bus: 21, 130, 131, 139, 145, 186. Admission charge

RETAIL THERAPY

Changi Airport So-called 'duty free' shopping at airports can be a scam but not, generally speaking, at Changi Airport. There are more than 100 shops in the departures and transit lounges of Terminals 1 and 2. Cutting Edge in Terminal 1 is good for gadgets and gizmos. ⓐ Changi Airport ⓛ 07.00–22.00

Rumah Bebe A specialist beadwork and embroidery shop where you can be tempted by beaded slippers or a complete Peranakan wedding costume. Beading demonstrations are usually available but phone to check on times.
🅐 113 East Coast Rd 🕓 6247 8781 🕒 09.30–18.30 Tues–Sun, closed Mon 🅝 MRT: Aljunied

TAKING A BREAK

Amigo £ At a weekend lunchtime it is not unusual to see a queue waiting for a dish of *laksa*, wanton noodles or *chicken chop hor fun* from Amigo. 🅐 01-05 Changi Village Food Centre 🕒 09.00–20.00 🅝 Bus: 2 from Victoria St or Tanah Merah to Changi Village

Mei Xiang Goreng Pisang Popiah £ This is the outlet to head for if you want delicious banana fritters cooked on the spot. The outlet at 01-31 offers an alternative snack in the form of carrot cake but it does not look or taste like what you might expect.
🅐 01-15 Changi Village Food Centre 🕒 09.00–20.00 🅝 Bus: 2 from Victoria St or Tanah Merah to Changi Village

First Stop Restaurant £–££ There are a couple of other places to eat on Pulau Ubin, but this is the most popular restaurant, partly because it has the widest choice of seafood and favourites like black pepper steak and sweet and sour chicken. A cold beer after a hot cycle goes down well here too. 🅐 Pulau Ubin, on the road by the jetty 🕓 6543 2489 🕒 11.00–20.00 Thur–Tues, closed Wed 🅝 Bus: 2 from Victoria St or Tanah Merah to Changi Village, then a boat from the nearby Changi Ferry Terminal (07.00–19.00 to the island)

Salt Water ££ This is the most comfortable setting for an evening meal in Changi and there is usually a seafood buffet, with international-style food as well, most evenings of the week. ❷ Changi Village Hotel, 1 Netheravon Rd ❶ 6379 7111 ❸ 06.30–23.00 ❹ Bus: 2 from Victoria St or Tanah Merah to Changi Village

AFTER DARK

Long Beach Seafood Restaurant ££ A famous seafood restaurant on the east coast where fresh fish are scooped out of the tanks and air-flown crabs from Alaska arrive at the kitchen packed in ice. The menu is extensive but some of the most popular choices are the chilli crabs and the lobster. The bamboo clam dish is rather special as well. ❷ 1018 East Coast Parkway ❶ 6445 8833 ❻ www.longbeachseafood.com.sg ❸ 11.15–15.00, 17.00–23.45 ❹ Bus: 401

ACCOMMODATION

Hotel 81 Joo Chiat £–££ See page 38 for details of this excellent chain of budget-priced hotels. This one, on Joo Chiat Road, is not the most conveniently located for the city centre but the price difference would still allow for taxi rides, never mind public transport. ❷ 305 Joo Chiat Rd ❶ 6348 8181 ❻ www.hotel81.com.sg ❹ MRT: Eunos

Changi Village Hotel ££–£££ Describing itself as 'minimalist chic', this smart-looking hotel with 380 rooms does have an uncluttered feel; it also faces the sea and has a spa. Relax in the swimming pool and gaze upwards at the planes using nearby Changi Airport. ⓐ Changi Village Hotel, 1 Netheravon Rd ❶ 6379 7111 ⓦ www.fareasthotels.com.sg ⓝ Bus: 2 from Victoria St or Tanah Merah to Changi Village

Nirwana Resort Hotel £££ A range of room types are available, along with a coffee shop, poolside restaurant, bistro and pub. You'll also find scuba diving, a gym and a jogging track. The contact information below also covers sister resorts including the similarly priced **Mayang Sari** and the five-star **Indra Maya**. ⓐ Bintan Island ❶ Reservations: 6323 6636 ⓦ www.nirwanagarden.com ⓝ Ferries from Tanah Merah Ferry Terminal (❶ 6542 4369 ⓦ www.brf.com.sg ● 09.05–20.15 Mon–Thur, 08.05–20.00 Fri, 08.05–20.00 Sat & Sun)

● *There are several tourist information centres to choose from*

PRACTICAL
information

Directory

GETTING THERE

By air

Changi Airport (☎ 6542 1122 ⓦ www.changi.airport.com.sg) is your most likely arrival point in the city. It has links to all major airports and is served by most major airlines as well as some local budget companies. Flying time from London is 13 hours, New York 18, Los Angeles 18 and Sydney 8.

Many people are aware that air travel emits CO_2, which contributes to climate change. You may be interested in lessening the environmental impact of your flight through Climate Care, which offsets your CO_2 by funding environmental projects around the world. Visit ⓦ www.climatecare.org

AIRLINES IN SINGAPORE

Air France ☎ 6737 6355 ⓦ www.airfrance.com
American Airlines ☎ 800 616 2113 ⓦ www.aa.com
British Airways ☎ 6589 7000 ⓦ www.ba.com
Malaysian Airlines ☎ 6336 6777
ⓦ www.malaysiaairlines.com.my
Qantas ☎ 6589 7000 ⓦ www.qantas.com.au
Silk Air ☎ 6225 4488 ⓦ www.silkair.com
Singapore Airlines ☎ 6223 8888 ⓦ www.singaporeair.com
United Airlines ☎ 6873 3533 ⓦ www.united.com

By sea

Several cruise ships arrive at the HarbourFront terminals. There are also ferries from the Indonesian islands which dock at the Tanah Merah Ferry Terminal (see page 117) or the HarbourFront terminals. From Tioman on the east coast of Malaysia ferries arrive at the Tanah Merah Ferry Terminal.

By train

Singapore is connected via KTM (ⓦ www.ktmb.com.my), the Malaysian rail service, to Malaysia and Thailand. The train station is at Keppel Road (ⓣ 6222 5156). Cab or bus 97 brings you into the city.

By road

Singapore is linked to Malaysia by two causeways. Buses arrive at the Johor Bahru causeway, and final destinations in Singapore include the Golden Mile Complex and Lavender Street. Coach services to destinations in Malaysia and Thailand depart from these bus stations. An alternative cheaper means of road travel is to cross the causeway to Johor Bahru and take a bus from there.

ENTRY FORMALITIES

EU, US, Australian, New Zealand and Canadian citizens do not need a visa to enter Singapore. On arrival your passport will be stamped for a 14-day visit and you can ask for longer. Extensions for three months plus are possible through the Immigration Department. Another way to extend your stay in Singapore is to take a day trip into Johor Bahru. On return your passport will be stamped for another 14-day period.

You can bring into Singapore 1 litre of spirits, 1 litre of wine and 1 litre of beer. Duty is payable on all tobacco brought into the state. These restrictions do not apply if you enter the country from Malaysia (🌐 www.customs.gov.sg).

MONEY

The Singapore dollar is divided into 100 cents. Notes come in denominations of S$2, S$5, S$10, S$20, S$50, S$100, S$500, S$1,000 and S$10,000. Coins are in denominations of 1, 5, 10, 20 and 50 cents and S$1. There are S$1 notes in circulation, but these are rare and 1 cent coins are being decirculated but are still legal tender.

🔺 *The local currency is Singapore dollars*

HEALTH, SAFETY & CRIME

There are very few health hazards to take into account when visiting Singapore. Water is safe to drink (it wouldn't dare not be!) and there are no inoculations required for entry.

If you are entering from an area where yellow fever is endemic, you may be asked to show proof of a recent vaccination against the disease. Hepatitis and typhoid inoculation might be worth considering, especially if you are travelling on to other destinations in Asia, and you should check that all your other vaccinations are up to date. Protection against malaria is not necessary in Singapore. Dengue fever is a minor risk in Singapore, especially in the fast disappearing rural areas of the state.

Mosquito repellent is an essential requirement if you intend to visit any of the country park areas. Drinking water should be carried at all times and a sunhat is essential (Singaporeans often use umbrellas in the sun), as is sunscreen.

If you are bringing children, any medication should be brought with you. The hospital services, while not cheap, are excellent.

🛈 Singapore does not have any reciprocal medical arrangements with other countries, so medical insurance is essential.

You will be as safe in Singapore as you are likely to be anywhere in the world. Pickpockets operate here but the usual precautions should keep you safe. Be aware of your valuables at all times and watch out for distractions – e.g. one person bumps into you while another helps themselves.

OPENING HOURS

Shopping centres open 09.30–21.30; banks 09.30–15.00 Mon–Fri and 09.30–12.30 Sat; and offices 08.30–17.00 Mon–Sat. Chinese temples operate more or less from dawn to dusk, while Hindu temples follow the same hours but close for an hour at noon. Mosques generally open 08.30–12.00 and 14.30–16.00.

TOILETS

Toilets, like drinking water, wouldn't dare be unclean. The best place to seek them out is in shopping malls, hotel lobbies, tourist sites, fast food outlets and hawker centres (although these can get a little messy because of the sheer volume of people using them). No one will mind or even notice you popping in. Most have at least one squat type toilet and you should carry tissues. There may be a charge of a few cents.

CHILDREN

Singapore is well aware of the spending power of children and there are any amount of activities to keep them busy. Just being around the wildlife in the parks and streets is fun, while the beaches and swimming pools are a blessed relief from shopping.

The food might have been designed with children in mind. Hawker centres are great fun, fast food outlets are thick on the ground and there are so many inexpensive local dishes to try out. Restaurants welcome children, most have child seats and many have child menus.

⬥ *Children love DUCKtours' novel bus-cum-boat ride*

Most tourist destinations have child reductions and hotels rarely charge a full rate for children under 12. There is no problem finding disposable nappies, baby food, bottles, etc.

The following are great places to take children:

Bukit Timah Nature Reserve (see page 117)
DUCKtours Take a ride around the city and its waterways in an amphibious vessel. Enquire with the same company about the DHL balloon ride, at time of visit located at Tan Quee Lan Street, Bugis Junction (11.00–22.00). ⓐ Suntec City ⓣ 6338 6877 ⓦ www.ducktours.com.sg ⓛ 10.00–18.00 ⓝ MRT: City Hall, then walk through Citylink Mall to Suntec City. Admission charge
East Coast Parkway Miles and miles of cycle paths, fast food places, rollerblades for hire, beaches, barbecues and more. ⓝ Bus: 401
Escape Theme Park Big amusement park at Pasir Ris with 17 different scary rides. ⓐ 1 Pasir Ris Close ⓣ 6581 9112 ⓦ www.escapethemepark.com.sg ⓛ 10.00–20.00 Sat, Sun & school holidays ⓝ MRT: Pasir Ris
HIPPOtours Hop-on hop-off open top bus travelling around the various sights of Singapore. Takes the strain out of sightseeing. Five different tours including evenings. ⓐ Suntec City ⓣ 6338 6877 ⓦ www.ducktours.com.sg ⓛ 10.00–17.30 city hop-on hop-off tour, 18.00–22.00 evening hop-on hop-off tour, 10.00–21.00 Sentosa hop-on hop-off tour ⓝ MRT: City Hall, then walk through Citylink Mall to Suntec City. Admission charge
Jurong Bird Park (see page 108)
Kart World Go-karting fun for those aged eight and over. ⓐ Behind KFC in Yung Ho Rd, Taman Jurong ⓣ 6266 2555

Ⓦ www.kartworld.com.sg Ⓛ 11.00–19.00 Tues–Sun
Ⓜ MRT: Lakeside, then bus 154. Admission charge

MINT Museum of Toys Five floors of vintage toys and, of course, a shop. ⓐ 26 Seah St ⓣ 6287 0060 Ⓦ www.emint.com
Ⓛ 09.30–18.30 Ⓜ MRT: City Hall. Admission charge

Pulau Ubin (see page 119)

Sentosa (see page 109)

Singapore Jet Boat One of many possibilities for a ride on the river. This one goes fast and does fancy moves. Minimum height of 1.3 m (4 ft). ⓐ One Fullerton Merlion Park ⓣ 9730 5053
Ⓦ www.singaporejet.com.sg Ⓛ 09.00–18.00 Tues–Sun
Ⓜ MRT: City Hall/Raffles Place. Admission charge

Singapore Science Centre (see page 111)

Sungei Buloh Wetland Park Choose from a number of walks, from 500 m (550 yards) to 7 km (4 miles), around this amazing nature reserve, to see mangroves and mangrove wildlife.
ⓐ 301 Neo Tiew Crescent ⓣ 6794 1401 Ⓦ www.sbwr.org.sg
Ⓛ 07.00–19.00 Mon–Sat, 07.30–19.00 Sun & public holidays
Ⓜ Bus: 925 from Kranji MRT station. Admission free on weekdays

Wild Wild Wet Right next door to the Escape Theme Park, this is a series of water rides, pools, etc. ⓐ 1 Pasir Ris Close ⓣ 6581 9128
Ⓦ www.wildwildwet.com Ⓛ 13.00–19.00 Mon, Wed–Fri, 10.00–17.00 Sat & Sun Ⓜ MRT: Pasir Ris. Admission charge

The Zoo (see page 119)

ⓘ Remember to keep children covered with sun hats and sunscreen, and make sure they have lots of water to drink. Mosquito repellent is essential in country and city parks.

COMMUNICATIONS

Telephones

Public telephones are located around the island and take either coins, phone cards or credit cards. A three-minute local call costs 10 cents. Coin phones take only small denomination coins and can mostly only be used for local calls. Cards for card phones come in denominations of S$3, S$5, S$10, S$20 and S$50, and can be bought at post offices and some shops. Used phone cards are highly collectible.

Mobile phones are widely used. If you have a GSM 900 or GSM 1800 phone, you can buy a prepaid SIM card to use while in Singapore.

TELEPHONING SINGAPORE

To telephone Singapore from abroad, dial the international access code first (00), then the country code for Singapore (65), followed by the eight-digit number.

TELEPHONING ABROAD

To make an international call from Singapore, dial 001, then the country code, followed by the local area code minus the first 0, and finally the number.

Country codes:

Australia 61

Canada & USA 1

New Zealand 64

Republic of Ireland 353

South Africa 27

UK 44

ℹ American mobile phone users will need to hire a phone or buy a second-hand one for use while in Singapore.

Three phone companies operate in Singapore; each has different rates for outgoing calls and mobile phone hire and rates:

M1 Ⓦ www.M1.com.sg
SingTel Ⓦ www.singtel.com
Starhub Ⓦ www.starhub.com

Internet

Internet cafés are becoming rare in Singapore (as in other countries) since everyone is connected to broadband at home, work or school. Libraries have Internet stations, and Starbucks, McDonald's, Coffeebean cafés and other locations have free wireless connection. Some public areas of the city also have wireless connection.

Post office

The main post office is at Eunos Road 8, but there are sub post offices in most of the big shopping centres. The Eunos Road PO has a poste restante. Airmail letters start at S$1.10 and postcards cost 50 cents. 🕐 08.30–17.00 Mon–Fri, 08.30–13.00 Sat.
ℹ 1606 for the nearest branch to you
(Ⓦ www.singpost.com).

ELECTRICITY

Mains electricity is 220–240 V 50 Hz. Plugs are uniformly three square pins, although lots of electrical appliances come with a two-pin plug. Adaptors are readily available.

TRAVELLERS WITH DISABILITIES

Travellers with disabilities will do fairly well in Singapore. Most modern hotels have wheelchair access and specially designed rooms, although advance notice is necessary to get one. The MRT might prove a problem for wheelchair users, but most shopping centres have ramps and lifts. Road crossings have an aural signal as well as a visual one.

Visit Ⓦ www.dpa.org.sg – a useful website to check before arriving. It lists cinemas, shopping centres and many other places with an account of their facilities for travellers with disabilities. Smart Taxis (Ⓣ 6555 8888 Ⓦ www.smrttaxis.com.sg) has London black cab-style taxis that need advance booking. Allow 24 hours at least.

FURTHER INFORMATION

Tourist offices

Changi Airport Ⓐ Arrivals lounge in Terminals 1 and 2 & transit hall in Terminals 1 and 2 Ⓛ 06.00–02.00 Ⓝ MRT: Changi

Cruise Centre Ⓐ Arrivals lounge, Cruise Centre, HarbourFront Ⓛ 24 hours Ⓝ MRT: HarbourFront

Liang Court Ⓐ 177 River Valley Rd, Level 1 Liang Court Shopping Centre Ⓛ 10.30–21.30 Ⓝ MRT: Clarke Quay

Little India Ⓐ 73 Dunlop St Ⓛ 10.00–22.00 Ⓝ MRT: Little India

Orchard ⓐ Junction of Orchard Rd & Cairnhill Rd
🕑 09.30–22.30 Ⓝ MRT: Orchard
Suntec ⓐ The Galleria, Suntec City Mall 🕑 10.00–18.00
Ⓝ MRT: City Hall
24-hour tourist hotline ⓣ 1800 736 2000 within Singapore and
65 6736 2000 outside Singapore ⓦ www.visitsingapore.com

BACKGROUND READING

David Brazil, *Street Smart Singapore* (Times Editions). Lots of
fascinating stories about the city state.

Connie Clarkson, *Asian Flavours* (New Holland). Singaporean
hawker-style recipes.

James Clavell, *King Rat* (Flame 1999). Account of the misery of
survival in Changi prisoner of war camp.

JG Farrell, *Singapore Grip* (Phoenix, 1996). Novel set in pre-
Japanese occupied Singapore.

Nick Leeson, *Rogue Trader* (Time Warner, 1999). Account by the
infamous rogue trader of his exploits in Singapore.

Lee Geok Boi, *The Syonan Years* (National Archives of Singapore,
2005). A very readable and generously illustrated book about
Singapore during World War II.

Emergencies

Your closest encounter with crime may occur when you commit one yourself. Jaywalking, smoking in certain places, spitting, eating on the MRT, chewing gum, urinating in lifts and littering are all offences that can incur an on-the-spot fine. Don't be confused by seeing Singaporeans jaywalking, littering or smoking and thinking that these laws are not imposed. Buggery, even between consenting adults in the privacy of their own home, is also illegal although the gay scene is an active and lively one.

❶ Overstaying your time on the island and possessing fireworks incur a caning, and having even tiny amounts of drugs incurs a long jail sentence. Drug trafficking is punished by the death penalty. Even having residual amounts of drugs in your system, consumed before entry to the state, is illegal.

EMERGENCY NUMBERS
Police ❶ 999
Ambulance and fire brigade ❶ 995

Hospital 24-hour emergency assistance
A&E departments are open 24 hours.
Alexandra Hospital ⓐ Alexandra Rd ❶ 6472 2000
Gleneagles ⓐ 6A Napier Rd ❶ 6470 5700
Mount Alvernia ⓐ 820 Thomson Rd ❶ 6347 6210
Mount Elizabeth ⓐ 3 Mount Elizabeth ❶ 6731 2218
Raffles Hospital ⓐ 585 North Bridge Rd ❶ 6311 1555
Singapore General Hospital ⓐ Outram Rd ❶ 6321 4311

EMERGENCIES ⓘ

Other useful numbers
Complaints hotline ☎ 1800 736 3366 (toll free)
Flight information ☎ 1800 542 4422 (toll free)
Drug & Poison Information Centre ☎ 6423 9119 (toll free)
STB complaints hotline ☎ 1800 736 3366 (toll free)
Touristline ☎ 1800 736 2000 (toll free)

Lost or stolen credit cards
American Express ☎ 6880 1111
Mastercard ☎ 800 110 0113
Visa ☎ 800 448 1250

Consulates & embassies
Australia @ 25 Napier Rd ☎ 6836 4100
Canada @ 15th Floor IBM Tower, 80 Anson Rd ☎ 6325 3240
UK @ 100 Tanglin Rd ☎ 6424 4200
USA 27 Napier Rd ☎ 6476 9100

SPOTA CITY IN SECONDS

This great range of pocket city guides will have you in the know in no time. Lightweight and packed with detail on the most important things from shopping and sights to non-stop nightlife, they knock spots off chunkier, clunkier versions. Titles include:

Amsterdam	Bratislava	Glasgow	Madrid	Seville
Antwerp	Bruges	Gothenburg	Marrakech	Singapore
Athens	Brussels	Granada	Milan	Sofia
Bangkok	Bucharest	Hamburg	Monte Carlo	Stockholm
Barcelona	Budapest	Hanover	Munich	Strasbourg
Belfast	Cardiff	Helsinki	Naples	St Petersburg
Belgrade	Cologne	Hong Kong	New York	Tallinn
Berlin	Copenhagen	Istanbul	Nice	Tokyo
Bilbao	Cork	Kiev	Oslo	Turin
Bologna	Dubai	Krakow	Palermo	Valencia
	Dublin	Kuala Lumpur	Palma	Venice
	Dubrovnik	Leipzig	Paris	Verona
	Dusseldorf	Lille	Prague	Vienna
	Edinburgh	Lisbon	Porto	Vilnius
	Florence	Ljubljana	Reykjavik	Warsaw
	Frankfurt	London	Riga	Zagreb
	Gdansk	Los Angeles	Rome	Zurich
	Geneva	Lyon	Salzburg	
	Genoa		Sarajevo	

The publishers would like to thank the following organisations for providing their copyright photographs for this book:
© Photographer: Alvin Teo/Agency: Dreamstime.com page 128; Singapore DUCKtours Pte Ltd page 131; Flickr pages 91 (Bernard Tey), 117 (Modery); Pat Levy pages 9, 19, 25, 29, 30, 39, 40, 50, 59, 61, 73, 77, 86, 125; Pictures Colour Library pages 1, 21, 23, 42–3, 45, 48, 103; Courtesy of Singapore Tourism Board pages 7, 10, 14, 27, 35, 46, 109; Wikimedia page 66 & 82 (Terence Ong), 94 (Sengkang), 104 (CalvinTeo), 120 (Terence Ong); World Pictures page 32.

Copy editor: Sandra Stafford
Proofreader: Emma Sangster

Send your thoughts to
books@thomascook.com

- **Found a great bar, club, shop or must-see sight that we don't feature?**

- **Like to tip us off about any information that needs updating?**

- **Want to tell us what you love about this handy little guidebook and more importantly how we can make it even handier?**

Then here's your chance to tell all! Send us ideas, discoveries and recommendations today and then look out for your valuable input in the next edition of this title.

Send an email to the above address (stating the book's title) or write to: CitySpots Project Editor, Thomas Cook Publishing, PO Box 227, The Thomas Cook Business Park, Unit 18, Coningsby Road, Peterborough PE3 8SB, UK.